STAYING POSITIVE
IN A NEGATIVE WORLD

Attitudes That Enhance the Joy of Living

ROGER CAMPBELL

Kregel
Publications

To
Jeremiah and Shiloh
Our first grandson and grandaughter

Staying Positive in a Negative World: Attitudes That Enhance the Joy of Livinig

Copyright © 1984, 1997, 2009 by Roger Campbell

Published by Kregel Publications, a division of Kregel, Inc., P.O. Box 2607, Grand Rapids, MI 49501. Kregel Publications provides trusted, biblical publications for Christian growth and service. Your comments and suggestions are valued.

Library of Congress Cataloging-in-Publication Data
Campbell, Roger.
    Staying positive in a negative world / Roger Campbell.
        p.   cm.
    Originally published: Wheaton, Ill. : Victor Books, 1984.
    1. Christian life. I. Title.
BV4501.2.C2475   1997   248.4—dc21   96-46391
                                                                    CIP

ISBN 978-0-8254-2427-4

Printed in the United States of America
3 4 5 / 13 12 11

Table of Contents

Introduction   **7**

1   God Really Cares   **9**

2   Faith Drives the Clouds Away   **18**

3   Reprogramming   **28**

4   No Time for the Pits   **38**

5   Can't Afford the Money Blues   **49**

6   Look for the Best in Others   **59**

7   Take the Long Look   **69**

8   Don't Look Back   **79**

9   The Secret of Contentment   **89**

10   Health and Happiness   **98**

11   You're Dynamite   **107**

12   Do Something!   **117**

Introduction

The Sunday morning service had just ended.

Members of the congregation were filing out of the church, shaking hands and exchanging greetings. I had never ministered here before but felt at ease with the people. The bond of love between us was new but familiar.

One of the worshipers stopped to ask me if I might consider writing something to help those struggling with negative attitudes.

"I'm so negative," he said. "I'm negative about the church—about everything."

Earlier, I had been working on an outline for a book intended to aid those who were having trouble with this very problem. Now here was a confirmation of my conviction that help was needed.

Millions who exit church services and others who never enter them are defeated by this destructive attitude. Negativism is a thief, robbing life of adventure and joy. This enemy affects every institution of society. It weakens families; it slows down churches in their outreach; even the economy of the nation is drained of needed vitality by this crippling condition that causes its victims to expect little and attempt less.

I wrote *Staying Positive in a Negative World* for those who are tired of being down, tired of despair, tired of clouds, and tired of valleys.

There is a better way to live.

Positively.

1

God Really Cares

The year was 1929. J.C. Penney was a patient in the Kellogg Sanitarium in Battle Creek, Michigan. He was broken in health and filled with despair.

Getting out of bed one night, he wrote farewell letters to his wife and son, saying he did not expect to live to see the dawn. But the next day brought an experience that changed Penney's life and restored his health. Let him tell it:

> When I awoke the next morning, I was surprised to find that I was still alive. Going downstairs, I heard singing in a little chapel where devotional exercises were held each morning. I can still remember the hymn they were singing, "God Will Take Care of You." Going into the chapel, I listened with a weary heart to the singing, the reading of the Scripture lesson, and the prayer. Suddenly—something happened. I can't explain it. I can only call it a miracle. I felt as if I had been instantly lifted out of the darkness of a dungeon into warm, brilliant sunlight. I felt as if I had been transported from hell to paradise. I felt the power of God as I never had felt it before. I realized that God with His love was there to help me. From that day to this, my life has been free from worry.[1]

Penney's chapel lesson dispelled his fears and prepared him for a bright and successful future as founder of the department store chain bearing his name. He had learned that God really cares.

But this can be a difficult lesson to learn.

Reacting to Trouble

We live in a troubled world. And trouble comes to all. If our conception of God's care is dependent on the circumstances at hand, we may find ourselves doubting His love.

Few people have difficulty believing that God cares when things are going well. But things do not always go well. Jesus said, "In the world ye shall have tribulation" (John 16:33).

How do you react when trouble comes?

Do you become pessimistic? Depressed? Angry with God?

In his excellent article, "Pulling through Depression," published in *Moody Monthly,* Craig Massey says: "Often the believer deepens his depression by isolating himself from the Lord. He says, in essence, 'I don't believe You are with me. I don't believe you care. I don't believe You hear me.' "[2]

This kind of response to trouble is not just a product of these tense times. It is characteristic of the nature of man and has surfaced in times of trial through the centuries.

Doubting God's Care

Standing at the Red Sea with Pharaoh's army in hot pursuit, the Children of Israel doubted God's care. Fear caused them to question His goodness and love. Though they had witnessed His power and protection in their deliverance from slavery in Egypt, they now buckled under pressure. Concluding that God had forsaken them, they accused Moses of having taken them into the wilderness to die (Ex. 14:10-12).

Shortly after their tirade against Moses, one of the greatest miracles of the Old Testament took place: the Red Sea opened before them, allowing their safe passage to freedom. This caused their faith to soar and gave them a song.

But three days later, the only water they could find was bitter and undrinkable. They were in the pits.

Still patient with His people, God sweetened the waters of Marah and confirmed His promises to them, guaranteeing His continued care (Ex. 15:23-27).

They were on top of the world.

A short time later they ran out of food and the cloud of gloom moved in again. This time they not only complained against their leaders but insisted it would have been better for them to have died during the plagues that had come to Egypt when God was securing their freedom (Ex. 16:2-3).

Every time trouble came they began looking back to Egypt. "If only—," they said.

God Meets Us

You may be looking back and second guessing decisions made in the past. You think things would be better "if only" you had not moved . . . or changed jobs . . . or married your mate. But looking back is futile . . . and unnecessary.

God meets us where we are.

He knew all about the hunger of His people and provided manna for them to eat. Had they been able to go back in time and reverse their decision to leave Egypt, they would have missed the experience of a lifetime: the single occasion on this planet when earth people ate angel's food.

Adversity also caused Job's wife to doubt God's care. When her husband was healthy and wealthy, it was easy for her to see God's hand in all their affairs. There is no record of even one negative word from her during their time of prosperity.

Then trouble came.

She and her husband lost everything, including their seven sons and three daughters. Finally Job's health went; he was covered with boils from head to foot. It was too much for this grieving woman. Reacting to changed circumstances, she concluded that God had forsaken them and blurted out her infamous statement: "Dost thou still retain thine integrity? Curse God, and die" (Job 2:9).

Mrs. Job may be the most maligned woman in the Bible. But her husband seems to respond to her one lapse into negativism tenderly, telling her that she is out of character, that she is speaking as one of the foolish women . . . not as she would have ordinarily spoken (Job 2:10).

The Pulpit Commentary makes the following observation about the disappointing outburst of Job's wife during the time of her deep depression:

> Men have been too hard on Job's wife for this one foolish saying of hers, forgetting how huge was her affliction. Indeed a great injustice has been done her, and while sympathy and admiration have been lavished on the husband, the partner in distress has scarcely received a glance of pity. But his troubles were her troubles. She had been in affluence, the happy mother of a happy family. Now she is plunged into poverty and misery, bereft of her children, with her once honored husband in disease and corruption. Is it wonderful (strange) that she should utter one hasty, impatient word?[3]

This is consistent with Job's response. After telling his wife that her reaction is not like her but like the foolish women, he explains that God's love is unchanged by their difficult circumstances (Job 2:10). His correct understanding of the situation is a mark of his spiritual maturity. The harshness of his wife's negative challenge under pressure, when she was not known for that kind of attitude, shows to what depths depression may drive us and emphasizes the importance of looking beyond the ash pits of life to our unchanging Lord.

The most familiar biblical example of believers doubting God's care under stress is that of the disciples during the storm on the Sea of Galilee (Mark 4:35-41). Having been instructed by Jesus to cross over to the other side, they started the journey without delay. Weary from the busy day's labor, the Saviour slept in the rear of the tossing boat.

Suddenly a great storm swept in upon them. Strong winds piled the waves high. The boat began taking on water, and they were in danger of going down.

The storm in this text pictures the storms of life through which we all pass from time to time, and the whole harrowing experience is loaded with practical lessons. Perhaps the most important of these is the truth that Christians have trials in life even when they are studying and applying God's Word and living lives of obedience to the Lord. Commenting on this time of peril for the disciples, J.C. Ryle has written:

Let us learn then, first of all, that following Christ will not prevent our having earthly sorrows and troubles.

Here are the chosen disciples of the Lord Jesus in great anxiety. The faithful little flock is allowed by the Shepherd to be much disquieted. The fear of death breaks in upon them like an armed man. Peter, James, and John, the pillars of the church about to be planted in the world, are much distressed.

Perhaps they had expected Christ's service would at any rate lift them above the reach of earthly trials. Perhaps they thought that He who could raise the dead, and heal the sick, and feed multitudes with a few loaves and fishes, and cast out devils with a word—He would never allow His servants to be sufferers on earth. Perhaps they had supposed He would always grant them smooth journeys, fine weather, an easy course, and freedom from trouble and care.

If the disciples thought so, they were much mistaken.[4]

Alarmed at their apparent peril, the disciples cried, "Master, carest Thou not that we perish?" (Mark 4:38). And their question reveals their problem to be the same as that of the troubled Israelites following Moses, Job's wife, and many today: in adversity they doubted His care.

Responding to their cry, Jesus arose and rebuked the wind and said to the sea, "Peace, be still" (v. 39). At His command, the wind ceased blowing and the sea flattened. There was a great calm. Then Jesus asked two probing questions: "Why are ye so fearful? How is it that ye have no faith?" (Mark 4:40)

These are good questions to ponder on our down days.

Afraid, the disciples raised a question of their own: "What manner of man is this, that even the wind and the sea obey Him?" (Mark 4:41)

They might have answered their own question: "He is a man who cares in a storm!"

Whatever your storm, if you belong to Him, He cares.

Proofs of God's Care

God's care is shown in His creation. Once, when Martin Luther felt depressed, he heard a bird singing its evening song. Then he saw it tuck its head under its wing and go to sleep. He said, "This little bird has had its supper and now is getting ready to go to sleep, quite content, never troubling itself as to what its food will be or where it will lodge on the morrow. Like David, it abides under the shadow of the Almighty. It sits on its little twig content and lets God care." The bird's example lifted Luther from despair and enabled him to get on with his important work.[5]

Jesus often appealed to lessons in nature to demonstrate God's care for His children. He spoke of birds that neither sow nor reap nor gather into barns but are fed of our heavenly Father (Matt. 6:26). And his message about the lilies of the field is one of the most comforting in the Bible for those enduring economic storms:

> And why take ye thought for raiment? Consider the lilies of the field, how they grow; they toil not, neither do they spin, and yet I say unto you that even Solomon in all his glory was not arrayed as one of these. Wherefore, if God so clothe the grass of the field, which today is, and tomorrow is cast into the oven, shall He not much more clothe you, O ye of little faith? (Matt. 6:28-30)

In his book, *Countdown,* G.B. Hardy points out a number of scientific facts about the earth and its relation to its atmosphere and other planets that demonstrate the Creator's care. He writes:

> We now know the size of our earth could not have been a thing of chance. It is exactly the right size for the sustenance of life. The height of the atmosphere is just right. . . . A change by as little as 10 percent either way in the size of our planet, and science agrees no life could exist. As a matter of absolute fact, life on earth is only possible because of an incredible number of "just rights."[6]

After listing a number of these "just rights," such as the atmosphere, the temperature, the amount of nitrogen and oxygen in the air, the earth's tilt, its speed of rotation and distance from the sun, he contrasts the earth to other planets as follows:

> These dead and dismal moons and planets are a witness to the providence and genius of God. They stand bleak in dazzling light or eternal blackness, in blistering heat or deadly cold. They stand an eternal witness to man of what his world would be like if a loving God had not meticulously fashioned it for life and comfort.[7]

Consider God's care the next time you see photographs of barren planets sent back from space. Look about you and understand that people are more important than any other part of God's creation.

While passing through a storm some years ago, I started the habit of looking out of my study window early in the morning, drinking in the view and saying, "Thank You, Lord, for allowing me to live in this beautiful place." I have found this a good way to start the day on a positive note. Appreciating the beauty that surrounds my home reminds me of God's mighty power, His great plan and His attention to minute details. There is a world of life all about us and that first look and my prayer of thanksgiving keeps me aware that my Father planned it all . . . and sustains it.

The early morning view from my window is always new. The seasons come and go, bringing color changes and different cycles of life that are peculiar to our area. Day after day, I am moved by the drama before me: the brilliant greens of spring, the reds and yellows of fall, the stark beauty of winter.

And there are the birds.

In the spring, robins and other warm weather lovers arrive with family plans in mind. I don't blame them for choosing this spot for nesting and raising their young. I have done the same.

Then there are times for watching larger varieties. Ducks become restless and start moving from one nearby lake to another. Some mornings, I will be greeted by the honking of Canadian geese in flight formation; always a wonder to me.

Finally, we will enter the time of cold winter storms. Except for the evergreens, the view from my window will be white. Many of the birds will have left with their kind for warmer places. Only the hardy ones will stay: bluejays, cardinals, sparrows . . . especially the sparrows, the common folk of the winged ones. And as I look at these busy brown customers awaiting my trip to the bird feeder, I remember that my heavenly Father cares about each one of them. If even one of them should perish in a winter blizzard, He will know about it (Matt. 10:29).

Shall I then think that any part of my life is unimportant to Him? Shall I doubt my Father's care when trouble comes? Never. We are of more value than many sparrows (Matt. 10:31). We can rest in His care.

God's care is most clearly seen in His provision for our salvation. Here is the greatest love story ever told: "For God so loved the world, that He gave His only begotten Son, that whosoever believeth in Him should not perish, but have everlasting life" (John 3:16).

Now here is a wonder: that we should think that God would care enough to make us citizens of heaven and then be disinterested in problems and heartaches that we encounter on our journey home.

Nothing could be further from the truth.

Everything about the Gospel declares God's continuing care for His own. Herbert Lockyer has written, "Justice demanded punishment for sin, and in His love God provided the One who should suffer death for every man. But His justice did not imperil His love and mercy. If a suffering heart is tempted to feel that God has not acted kindly or justly with him, let him remember Calvary."[8]

A woman who had endured excruciating pain while hospitalized with rheumatoid arthritis told me she had been able to stay on top during her suffering by remembering all that Jesus had endured on the cross. She knew her Lord would understand.

A minister who was being unjustly criticized by members of his congregation found strength to hold up under their bitter attacks by keeping his Saviour's suffering in mind. No one had injured him physically or cursed him publicly. He had not been crucified nor wronged as had his Master. Therefore, he could continue to stay positive while serving and even loving his persecutors.

C.H. Spurgeon wrote:

> God is with us in sorrows. There is no pang that rends the heart, I might almost say, not one which disturbs the body, but what Jesus Christ has been with you in it all. Feel you sorrows of poverty? He had no place to lay His head. Do you endure griefs of bereavement? Jesus wept at the tomb of Lazarus. Have you been slandered for righteousness' sake and has it vexed your spirit? Jesus said, "Reproach hath broken Mine heart." Have you been betrayed? Do not forget that He, too, had His familiar friend who sold him for the price of a slave.
>
> On what stormy seas have you been tossed which have not roared about His boat? Never glen of adversity so dark, so deep, apparently so pathless, but what, in stooping down, you may discover the footprints of the crucified One! In the fires and in the rivers, in the cold of night and under the burning sun, He cries, "I am with you; be not dismayed; for I am both thy Companion and thy God!"[9]

The Circle of God's Love

Negative attitudes overcome us when despair leads us to conclude that some areas of life lie outside the circle of God's love. This kind of thinking compartmentalizes God and limits expectation of His care. God's love, so clearly evident in creation and redemption, extends to all areas of life. All things that concern God's children concern their heavenly Father. "And we know that all things work together for good to them that love God, to them who are the called according to His purpose" (Rom. 8:28).

Are you passing through trials?

Are you hurting?

Our Lord has been where you are today.

"At the head of the procession of the world's sufferers is a thorn-crowned man."[10]

His name is Jesus.

He understands and cares.

2

Faith Drives the Clouds Away

Faith is positive. Doubt is negative. And there are doubt producers on every hand: hypocrisy, betrayal by those we trust, family problems, financial reverses, natural disasters, war, sickness, death.

To stay positive, I begin each day quoting Hebrews 11:1: "Now faith is the substance of things hoped for, the evidence of things not seen." Often I add Mark 9:23: "If thou canst believe, all things are possible to him that believeth." Being reminded of faith's power brings expectation to my day.

Dr. V. Raymond Edman, former president and late chancellor of Wheaton College, said: "Faith is dead to doubts, dumb to discouragements, blind to impossibilities, knows nothing but success. Faith lifts its hands up through the threatening clouds, lays hold of Him who has all power in heaven and on earth. Faith makes the uplook good, the outlook bright, the inlook favorable, and the future glorious."[1]

The Thrilling Possibilities of Faith

We should not be surprised to discover that faith exercised in daily life is the key to successful living. Eternal life comes through faith in Jesus Christ, and this same faith makes the abundant life that He promised a reality here and now (John 10:10). Spurgeon observed: "A little faith will bring your soul to heaven, but great faith will bring heaven to your soul."

As you read the Bible, you can't help being impressed by the thrilling possibilities of faith. The priests of Israel, bearing the ark of the covenant, step into the flooded Jordan River, and as they take that first step of faith, the waters upstream halt, allowing the entire nation to pass over from the wilderness to the Promised Land (Josh. 4). After six days of circling mighty Jericho, Joshua marches his army around the city seven times, and at a shout the walls fall down (Josh. 6). Young David spurns Saul's army to face the fearsome giant Philistine warrior Goliath, and with a few smooth stones, David is victorious over him (1 Sam. 17).

A woman who has been ill twelve years touches the hem of our Lord's garment and is instantly healed (Matt. 9:20-22). Two blind men follow the Saviour, crying out for mercy. He touches their eyes, saying, "According to your faith be it unto you," and they immediately receive their sight (Matt. 9:27-30). A troubled mother comes to Jesus seeking help for her demon-possessed daughter. Because of her great faith, her daughter is delivered that very hour (Matt. 15:28).

Ten years ago, my wife, Pauline, entered the hospital for treatment of what we thought was a severe case of the flu. Instead, it was discovered, she had been stricken with a life-threatening condition. For reasons still unknown, her blood had begun to destroy itself. Our doctor explained that she had become allergic to her own blood.

After receiving word of the seriousness of Pauline's condition, I returned from the hospital and walked through our home. Evidences of her loving work were everywhere: the pictures on the walls, the arrangement of the furniture, decoration of her own making—her special touch everywhere. My heart was heavy, and by the time I had finished my prayer tour, hot tears were burning trenches in my face.

Just at that point, the back door opened and our oldest son, David, entered the house. Seeing my tears, he put his arms around me, saying, "Don't worry, Dad. We're praying and everything will be fine. Have faith."

Faith.

How I needed it!

I had been with others many times when the lives of their loved ones were on the line and had encouraged them to believe, but this was different. It is one thing to exhort and another to experience.

During the difficult days that followed, I was moved by the promise given in Matthew 17:20: "If ye have faith as a grain of mustard seed, ye shall say unto this mountain, Remove hence to yonder place, and it shall remove; and nothing shall be impossible to you." This verse both challenged me and imparted hope. I longed to plumb its depths and harness its power.

I deeply appreciated the efforts of the doctors during this crisis, but apart from giving steroids and blood transfusions to sustain life, there seemed little that could be done. Faith offered another dimension for hope and brought a break in the clouds. I prayed earnestly and hundreds of others prayed with me.

Then came an encouraging phone call from our family doctor. He had thoughtfully instructed the person placing the call to immediately assure me that this call from his office was not to bring bad news. When he was finally on the line, his first words were, "Whatever you're doing, keep doing it!" Pauline's blood count was starting to rise.

Ten good years have passed since that fearful journey to death's door, and my wife has had no recurrence of the problem that brought her there. Our mountain has been removed. And we are grateful!

God Can Do Anything

Great faith is built on the conviction that God can do anything. Most Christians believe this, but few act on their belief. They accept omnipotence intellectually, but it makes little difference in their lives. Consequently, problems loom large, burdens become too heavy to bear, and they face the future with fear.

When Joel Carlson, 6' 4" center on the Grand Rapids Baptist College basketball team, went home to Coloma, Michigan for the Christmas holidays, he had no idea that the next few weeks would find him in the toughest contest in his life. He had planned to spend a relaxing break from school with his family, intending to join the basketball team for a trip to Ohio for tournaments beginning New Year's weekend.

Because a recent physical showed Joel's blood pressure had been a bit higher than normal, he visited his family doctor for what he expected would be a few routine tests. But the tests revealed that

Joel's heart had gone on a rampage, and he had unknowingly been walking a thin line between life and death for some time.

The problem with Joel's heart was one of irregular beating and fluttering. At times his heartbeat would increase to 240 beats a minute, and at other times it would decrease to 30 beats a minute. Sometimes it fluttered so rapidly that the blood wasn't being pumped through.

On New Year's Eve, he was admitted to Berrien General Hospital (near his home) and placed in the Cardiac Care Unit where his heart was monitored continuously. When his monitor set off an alarm that brought doctors and nurses rushing to his bed, he was surprised at all this concern. He had felt this way a number of times recently, even on the basketball court, without realizing his life was in jeopardy.

On the second day in the hospital, reality arrived. Joel's doctor told him he would probably never play basketball again. That was a bitter pill to swallow because it called for a whole new direction in his life. Joel's college major, physical education with a goal of coaching basketball, would have to be changed. And this was his senior year. Another shocker was the word that a pacemaker (an electrical device that stimulates the heart muscle so that it contracts at a certain or regular rate) seemed to be the only solution to the problem of keeping his heart in a normal rhythm.

A few months before Joel became ill, I had sent a copy of my book *Lord, I'm Afraid* to Joel's parents. Joel had read the book and had expecially noted my use of Jeremiah 32:27 as an antidote for fears about health when hope is slim: "Behold, I am the Lord, the God of all flesh: is there anything too hard for me?" Now, while his family, members of his home church, and many others prayed, he held to this powerful faith builder, believing that God was able to help him.

Hoping to avoid the implanting of a pacemaker, Joel's doctor treated him with medication intended to regulate his heart and bring it into proper rhythm; but Joel reacted to the treatment and developed a high fever, creating double trouble. The medication was then discontinued, and Joel was transferred to the University of Illinois Hospital in Chicago for more extensive testing by a specialist and a decision concerning the need of a pacemaker.

When Joel arrived at the hospital in Chicago, the peace of God had settled upon him and he was unafraid. Faith had taken his fears away. He also began to view the hospital as a mission field and saw every contact there as an opportunity to share faith in Christ.

When all of the testing had been completed, it was clear that a great change had taken place in Joel's body. God had honored his faith and had answered his prayers and those of his family and friends. His heart was now perfectly normal.

Joel was discharged from the hospital with the word from his doctor that he could do anything he wanted to do—even play basketball. Within a few weeks he was back to his starting position on the college team, a living demonstration that God can do anything.[2]

Since we live in a troubled world, there are many opportunities to exercise faith. These tight spots may come disguised as problems, but faith sees them as opportunities. Famous missionary Hudson Taylor once said that he liked to find himself in a corner so that he could see what God would do to get him out of it.

Faith Finds a Way

Faith adds a new dimension to consider when you face difficulties. When Thomas Edison began developing the phonograph, he grappled with many problems. The high tones were harsh and the low tones, muffled. Edison hired a man to help solve the problems, but after working for two years, the man went to Edison, discouraged and ready to give up on the project. Edison answered, "I believe that for every problem God has given us, He has a solution. We may not find it, but someday someone will. Go back and try a little longer."[3] We all know the results of that extra effort that grew out of Edison's faith in God's ability to reveal answers to all of the problems in life.

Faith provides an alternative.

In the most trying circumstances, faith finds another way.

When Jesus arrived at the home of Mary and Martha in Bethany, their brother, Lazarus, had died. Martha thought all hope was gone, saying, "Lord, if Thou hadst been here, my brother had not died" (John 11:21). Then her faith added another possibility: "But I know that even now, whatsoever Thou wilt ask of God, God will give it Thee" (John 11:22).

The Lord's response confirmed Martha's faith: "Thy brother shall rise again" (John 11:23).

But Martha's faith then wavered: "I know that he shall rise again in the resurrection at the last day," she replied (John 11:24).

At that point, Jesus challenged this grieving sister to let her faith soar, saying: "I am the resurrection and the life; he that believeth in Me, though he were dead, yet shall he live, and whosoever liveth and believeth in Me shall never die. Believest thou this?" (John 11:25-26)

Martha believed and her faith was rewarded.

In a short time, her brother, who had been dead four days, came walking out of the tomb at the call of Christ. Her Lord had kept His word. His promise had been worthy of her faith.

Thomas N. Carter, an ex-convict, told a thrilling story of his mother's faith. He had been wayward for many years and finally had been sent to prison. On one occasion while he was there, his mother received a telegram from the prison stating that he was dead and asking her what she wanted done with his body.

Carter's mother had prayed for years that he would one day be converted and become a preacher of the Gospel. Long hours on her knees with her heart filled with Bible promises had brought a confidence that God would answer her prayer. Now, stunned at the receipt of the telegram, she asked her family members not to disturb her while she spent time in prayer.

Opening the Bible, she placed the telegram beside it and began to pray. "O God," she said, "I have believed the promise You gave me in Your Word, that I would live to see Tom saved and preaching the Gospel, and now this telegram has come saying he is dead. Lord, which is true, this telegram or Your Word?"

When the faithful mother rose from her knees, having the assurance of God's answer, she wired the prison as follows: "There must be some mistake. My boy is not dead."

And there was a mistake. Tom Carter was alive, and when he finished his time in prison he became a preacher of the Gospel. A mother's faith had moved another mountain.[4]

Faith Grows with Exercise

Trials, then, are not the enemies of faith but are opportunities to prove God's faithfulness. George Müller, of Bristol, England, who became known worldwide for his faith because he prayed in millions of dollars for the support of orphans, called trials "the food of faith." He saw them as occasions to exercise faith. And to grow, faith needs exercising.

Müller wrote:

> Some say, "Oh, I shall never have the gift of faith Mr. Müller has got!" This is a mistake—it is the greatest error—there is not a particle of truth in it. My faith is the same kind of faith that all of God's children have had. It is the same kind that Simon Peter had, and all Christians may obtain like faith. My faith is their faith, though there may be more of it because my faith has been a little more developed by exercise than theirs; but their faith is precisely the faith that I exercise, only with regard to degree, mine may be more strongly exercised.[5]

The importance of exercising faith to develop it is seen in the experiences of Bible heroes. By the time Moses lifted his rod and parted the Red Sea, he had *already* witnessed the power of God in bringing the plagues upon Egypt. The falling of the walls in Jericho came *after* Joshua had led his people across the flooded Jordan River. David was able to face Goliath with confidence because *previously* he had conquered wild beasts that had attacked his father's sheep.

To increase your faith, start using the faith you now have. Do something that demands faith. Trust God to do something for you that no one else can do. Flex your spiritual muscles. Expect God to come through and to honor His commitments. You'll be thrilled with the results.

Faith Wins

Negative influences impact us daily. We experience physical and emotional pain, face conflicts with disagreeable people, receive unwanted bills in the mail, and ride past hospitals and cemeteries.

Weather changes are often not to our liking. Natural disasters strike, bringing destruction. Crime soars out of control, and international tensions seem to be moving us to the brink of nuclear holocaust.

Nor can we ignore the purpose of Satan to drag us down and defeat us. Job was healthy and wealthy before Satan launched his attack on him; but then he lost all he had. In spite of this, his cry from the ash pit still stands as a witness to his conquest of suffering through faith: "For I know that my Redeemer liveth, and that He shall stand at the latter day upon the earth" (Job 19:25).

Our faith will also make us triumphant in trouble: "For whatsoever is born of God overcometh the world, and this is the victory that overcometh the world, even our faith" (1 John 5:4). This faith is even sufficient for times of satanic attack and oppression: "Ye are of God, little children, and have overcome them; because greater is He that is in you, than he that is in the world" (1 John 4:4).

But the faith that wins and moves mountains does not rest in itself. Instead, it is anchored securely in God, who is faithful. Strong faith would be worthless if the object of our faith were not strong.

Faith's Resting Place

Standing on the bank of the Mississippi River, I looked up at the break in the bridge that spanned the river not far away. A large truck had been too much for the structure, and a section of it had given way just after the fortunate truck driver had crossed safely to the other side.

There had been nothing wrong with the truck driver's faith, for he had risked all in making that crossing. But the bridge was not worthy of his faith. Though he escaped with his life, the bridge was broken by the load placed upon it.

Our Lord is unlike that broken bridge.

He will not fail.

A Roman army officer came to Jesus seeking help for his servant who was sick of the palsy and in great pain. Jesus assured the man that he would come to his house and heal his servant. Upon hearing the Lord's promise, the officer replied: "Lord, I am not worthy that Thou shouldest come under my roof, but speak the word only, and my servant shall be healed. For I am a man under authority, having soldiers under me, and I say to this man, Go, and he goeth; and to another, Come, and he cometh; and to my servant, Do this, and he doeth it" (Matt. 8:8-9).

The Lord was moved by this officer's complete confidence in Him, saying: "I have not found so great faith, no, not in Israel" (Matt. 8:10).

The officer's faith was declared great because he believed that the power of Christ was great enough to meet his need. He saw no limit to our Lord's ability to respond to his request. His simple trust in the power of Christ amounted to great faith. As a result of his faith, his servant was healed.

Our faith grows in exact proportion to our confidence that God can do anything, and He can! "Ah Lord God! behold, Thou hast made the heaven and the earth by Thy great power and stretched out arm, and there is nothing too hard for Thee" (Jer. 32:17).

Dr. Len G. Broughton, a medical doctor, testified that a country preacher knocked out all of his skepticism in one sermon. Broughton had been unable to accept the miracle of the virgin birth of Christ.

Having begun his medical practice in a rural area, he attended a Sunday morning service being held in an old country meeting house. The preacher took the first verse of the Bible as his text and declared that this verse contained the only mysterious thing in the universe. He told his hearers if they could believe that God was there before the beginning, they could believe everything else in the Bible.

Dr. Broughton accepted the country preacher's logic and in that moment traded his doubts for faith. From that time on, his God was big enough to do anything.[6]

Regardless of your present situation, God is up to the occasion. He specializes in working in the dark. While doubts may be troubling you because of the enormity of your problem and your inability to come up with a solution, remember that faith finds another way. By exercising faith, your present adversity may become your greatest adventure.

In her helpful poem, "To Walk by Faith," Wava Campbell compares walking by faith to walking by sight. She describes our choices well:

> To walk by faith is such a great adventure;
> It thrills the spirit every passing day;
> To see God's hand, to know whatever happens,
> He understands and He will lead the way.
>
> To walk by sight is something very tragic;
> It makes the spirit droop, the heart grow cold.

It makes the Christian plan and fume and fumble;
It makes his body feel so tired and old.

Just how to walk life's road is our decision.
God leaves the choice with us and us alone.
But if we choose to walk by sight, we'll see not.
By faith His will is seen and felt and known.[7]

3

Reprogramming

"Oh, Pastor, you're always praising the Lord and talking about the victories, but you're not hearing what I'm hearing." The speaker was a member of my church.

"Praise the Lord!" I replied.

The few negatives that were evidently floating around among some members of my congregation at that time could not have been too serious. I continued as the pastor there for ten years after that conversation, and those were some of the greatest years of my life. Our church facilities were outgrown, necessitating a large building program, and two branch churches were established. Had I allowed the downers to deter me, I am confident that my service for the Lord would have been hindered and my ability to help others lessened. Defeat would have been snatched from the jaws of victory.

Actually, my concerned parishioner soon saw the light. Later, he came to tell me that he had isolated the source of the negativism that had been disturbing him. It centered in one family. As long as he limited his time with them, he could stay positive. When he spent more time in their company, he was influenced by their chronic complaining. As a result, he decided to associate with people who were a positive influence on him. His experience had taught him a valuable lesson: *TOO MUCH NEGATIVE INPUT CAN BE HAZARDOUS TO SPIRITUAL HEALTH.*

Some Needed Negatives

Now, of course, there are some proper negatives in life, even the Christian life. As the salt of the earth and the light of the world (Matt. 5:13-16), we must be opposed to some things. Part of right living is refusing to do wrong; to live a godly life, one must reject ungodliness: "The fear of the Lord is to hate evil" (Prov. 8:13).

Christians are citizens of another world while passing through this one (Phil. 3:20). And that presents some problems.

We are surrounded by worldly enticements and influences, but we must not set our hearts on them. Being pilgrims and strangers on earth (1 Peter 2:11), we are called to love things above (Col. 3:2). John warns, "Love not the world, neither the things that are in the world. If any man love the world, the love of the Father is not in him" (1 John 2:15).

Some Christians have interpreted separation from the world to mean only that they must abstain from certain activities labeled "worldly." That concept misses the point; it omits the positive side of separation.

Those who make dedication to Christ their main focus in life will have little trouble dropping improper activities. When one loves Christ supremely, proper negatives fall into place because the believer is so occupied with his Lord that the world loses its attraction. It is not legalism but love for Christ that makes the Christian life dynamic.

Don't Accentuate the Negative

Giving too much attention to negatives causes one to become an expert at faultfinding. The eloquent T. de Witt Talmage wrote of such chronic complainers: "I lay this down as a rule without exception, that those people who have the most faults themselves are the most merciless in their watching of others."[1]

Complaining Christians seldom see this solemn truth: their constant faultfinding is actually directed past the objects of their griping straight to the throne of God.

To complain about our circumstances is to complain about God, since He directs or allows the events that come into our lives.

Discontents are never dynamic witnesses. They may be effective at calling attention to problems or dividing believers, but they lack the power that love brings to the Christian life and to all Christian service (1 Cor. 13). They are unhappy about many things because they are dissatisfied with the One who is in charge of all things.

Complaining is an act of rebellion. But how can a person break the complaining habit? How can he learn to reject negativism? How can he become a positive person?

By reprogramming.

He must change his thought patterns.

This is what Paul had in mind when he taught the believers in Philippi how to have and keep the peace of God. He advised:

> Be careful (anxious) for nothing, but in everything by prayer and supplication with thanksgiving let your requests be made known unto God. And the peace of God, which passeth all understanding, shall keep your hearts and minds through Christ Jesus. Finally, brethren, whatsoever things are true, whatsoever things are honest, whatsoever things are just, whatsoever things are pure, whatsoever things are lovely, whatsoever things are of good report, if there be any virtue, and if there be any praise, think on these things (Phil. 4:6-8).

Talk about positive thinking! Here it is in a totally biblical setting. Yet many Christians ignore this clear instruction.

Wise Solomon explained that we are what we think (Prov. 23:7). One cannot therefore nurture negative thoughts and become a positive person.

Avoiding Negative Influences

But how can we avoid being controlled by the negative influences that surround us and confront us every day?

Consider these suggestions:

• *Reduce your intake of news.* We are the most informed people ever to live on the earth, and this is a heavy load to bear.

In former years, the average person largely concerned himself with events in his local community. Today, we have the dubious privilege of knowing about nearly everything that is wrong with the world every day. We are plugged into the news gathering services of the entire planet, and if not careful, we will find ourselves carrying burdens enough to break us down.

Not only is world news available, it pours into willing minds almost continually. Upon waking, you can catch the early morning news as you hurry through breakfast. At noon, lunch can be seasoned with all the violence of the first half of the day, tidbits of which have been reported at least hourly all morning. Following dinner, reporters and camera people describe events in as hair raising a manner as possible, disturbing your digestion—unless you desert them.

If you decide to relax with a few hours of light television viewing, expect periodic interruptions with up-to-the-minute reports intended to whet your appetite for the late news summary. Finally, just before retiring, you can watch a rerun of the murder and mayhem of the day so that you will be awake to all the misery of the world. Probably this will include a report of international tensions contributing to the accelerating arms race that will remind you of the nightmarish possibility of a nuclear war breaking out either by accident or design while you sleep.

At one time, I was so hooked on being in touch with every late-breaking event that the tuning buttons on my car radio were set to allow me to hear the latest news reported as often as possible by those whom I felt were most able to keep me well informed. By periodically pushing the right buttons, I could feel current with the world whenever I was driving.

Then, while passing through a time of great stress, I suddenly realized that part of my trouble was of my own making. I was feeding my fears by always reaching out for all the trouble I could grasp. As a result, I reset my radio buttons and started tuning out much of what I had formerly been inviting into my mind. The positive results of this move proved pleasantly surprising.

My decision to stop taking a daily newspaper for a time proved to be another productive experience. While preparing to write a book on fear, I tried this as an experiment, reasoning that some good should come from eliminating my intake of reported violence. That was five years ago, and I have not taken a daily newspaper since. Extreme? Perhaps—but it helps me, and think of the money I have saved!

Last year, while speaking in a church, I told about my decision to stop taking daily newspaper delivery and how pleased I had been with the results. Following the service, a woman came to tell me that she had been suffering from many fears and that she was going to try my suggestion and see if it made any difference. A few months later I talked with her and she joyfully told me that her anxieties were gone.

Don't misunderstand me!

Cutting back on news intake does not mean that we are to go through life with our heads in the sand. I generally read a news magazine weekly as well as a local weekly newspaper that features community happenings. Daily, I catch at least one television news program. From time to time, I pick up a daily newspaper, especially when there is something being reported in which I have a special interest.

But I am now in charge of my news intake. I can limit myself to sections of the newspaper or news items that I believe will be profitable to me. I am no longer a news-junkie. When it comes to the news that enters my mind, I am the anchorman. And I intend to keep it that way.

• *Eliminate negative entertainment.* Develop a selective eye for what you read and view. Stop listening and watching things that affect you negatively.

A family once asked me to visit their grandmother who was in the hospital. Upon entering Grandmother's hospital room, I found her reading a book, but the cover on this paperback was a scorcher!

She quickly covered the book, clearly embarrassed that I had come to visit while she was reading it. I fear that I ruined Grandmother's day, and that experience may have caused her to think negatively about ministers. But the real reason for her unpleasant experience was the book she had chosen to read during her stay in the hospital.

Any activity, entertainment, recreation, or pastime that violates your convictions produces an inner conflict that causes negative feelings. If you feel guilty about what you watch, read, or do, you will become negative about yourself (1 John 3:20). Your self-esteem will nosedive. Grieving the Holy Spirit in this manner will rob you of the peace of mind that comes from continually yielding to His control (Eph. 4:30). And you will be the loser.

Read wholesome books.

Limit television viewing to those programs that leave you feeling positive, challenged, encouraged, optimistic. But you may have trouble finding them on some channels!

Choose activities that are consistent with your Christian convictions and that you would be comfortable doing at our Lord's return (1 John 2:28).

• *Stop listening to those who are negative about others.* In his book, *How to Win over Depression,"* Tim LaHaye warns:

> There is no place in the Christian's life for negativism. Linked as we are with the divine power of God, we should never anticipate anything but success. Avoid the complainer, the griper and the critic; most of all avoid imitating them.
>
> Negativism, pessimism, griping, criticism, and gossip are not only harmful but also contagious. In fact you reinforce them in your mind every time you verbalize them. Keep your conversation *and* your mind positive at all times.[2]

In Critical Condition

A brokenhearted Christian wife shared with me reasons for her frustration. Things were not good in her home. And a group from her church spent much time complaining about their church and pastor. Nearly every social outing turned into a gossip time to eat away at the servant of God and his ministry. Times of fellowship that should have been uplifting were given to rehashing all the negative things discussed at the last meeting and adding new ones. Though this woman had not taken part in these slander sessions, she was being adversely affected by hearing others making negative comments over and over again.

Negativism is often like an epidemic. Sometimes its spread is almost impossible to contain. Negative thoughts and words about one subject can spill over into other areas that seem totally unrelated. In the above case, the poison being spewed in a small group of church grumblers was now threatening a marriage. By downgrading the church and pastor, this griping group was destroying the foundation on which this one troubled couple had built their home.

Shun the grumbling crowd.

Refuse to listen to harmful gossip.

Positive Resources

• *You will also want to deepen your devotional life.* Eliminating the negative will not be enough. You must accentuate the positive. And the Bible is God's positive message to hurting people.

Remember, faith is positive, and the Bible is the source of faith: "So then faith cometh by hearing, and hearing by the word of God" (Rom. 10:17).

• *Believers who get the most out of the Christian life and stay positive regularly attend church.* A few years ago, many "experts" were predicting the demise of organized churches, but the predictions failed because local churches are in God's plan for His people in this age. The Bible names church officers and clearly defends their duties.

The duty of a pastor is to keep you positive. See how this is revealed in Ephesians 4:11-12: "And he gave some, apostles; and some, prophets; and some, evangelists; and some, pastors and teachers; for the perfecting of the saints, for the work of the ministry, for the edifying of the body of Christ."

God's plan calls for your pastor and other church leaders to aid you in Christian growth so that you can do the work of the ministry and build up the body of Christ. But when you are negative and critical you certainly cannot minister to needy people and be a blessing to the church. God is then responsible to supply your pastor with wisdom and spiritual insights that will lead you to higher ground and make you a useful Christian able to set a positive example for others. God will do His part—but if you are not regular in church attendance, you will miss many blessings intended for you.

A pastor made this statement in a meeting when I was present: *"Christians are either problem conscious or power conscious."* That concise analysis has benefited me for twenty years. I cannot tell you how many times those eight words have caused me to focus on God's power rather than on my problems. But if I had missed that meeting I would not have heard that wise statement and my absence would have had a negative effect upon my life.

• *Personal Bible study and prayer also contribute greatly to a positive outlook.* In counseling troubled people, I have discovered the most revealing question to ask is: "How is your devotional life?" In almost every case of defeat or depression, a weak devotional life has been one of the causes.

How does one build a strong devotional life?

That, of course, varies with individuals. Devotional habits that work well for some may be impractical for others. Work schedules, school responsibilities, and even whether one is a morning or night person can all be factors. D.L. Moody often rose at 4 o'clock in the morning for prayer and Bible study, but some trying to imitate him might find themselves exhausted by noon and worthless the remainder of the day. We must be careful about trying to pour ourselves into the molds of others.

Perhaps the most important thing to keep in mind about devotional Bible reading is that it should be an experience in learning to feed ourselves. Devotional guides help, and I recommend their use; but we should not be satisfied with receiving all of our spiritual food from others. These aids should be but springboards from which we plunge into Bible study on our own.

I benefit from reading through books of the Bible. I search for faith-building verses, underlining them and enjoying their encouragement. I then write them on a card to keep on my desk or carry with me through the day.

Sometimes after reading my chosen text, I browse through other books of the Bible to be refreshed by verses that I have previously underlined. I call this drinking at favorite fountains. Often these familiar verses that have kept me positive in other times are just what I need for the challenges facing me now.

Prayer is all too often neglected as a positive resource for Christians. Waiting quietly before God silences negative voices. Asking God for provision, power, and guidance increases expectation. The amount of peace we experience in prayer depends on how many of our concerns we place in the loving hands of God.

R.A. Torrey said, "Prayer promotes our spiritual growth as almost nothing else, indeed as nothing else but Bible study; and true prayer and Bible study go hand in hand."[3]

While it is important to have a definite time each day for personal devotions, it is equally important to take a devotional attitude with us through each day. It is one thing to be positive in a quiet place with an open Bible and quite another to be quietly positive in the stress of daily living. Whatever our circumstances, let us remember that as believers we are equipped to cope. A.W. Tozer wrote:

> Of one thing we may be sure, we can never escape the external stimuli that cause vexation. The world is full of them, and though we were to retreat to a cave and live the remainder of our days alone, we still could not lose them. The rough floor of our cave would chafe us, the weather would irritate us, and the very silence would cause us to fret.
>
> Let us look out calmly upon the world; or better yet, let us look down upon it from above where Christ is seated and we are seated with Him.[4]

In addition to suggestions already mentioned to help you stay positive, lets quickly consider other ways. In this electronic age, faith may be encouraged through listening to Christian radio stations, viewing Christian television programs, or hearing recorded faith builders in song or word.

Looking for Help

Being on the lookout for positive stimuli can add a whole new dimension to living. And there are thrilling sights and sounds all around us.

Hear birds instead of sirens.

Hear laughter instead of complaining.

See the beauty of snowflakes instead of complaining about the depth of the snow.

Look for rainbows instead of dark rain clouds.

This morning I found myself noticing the height of some evergreen trees on a hill near our home. Standing well above the trees around them, these giants reminded me that they never lose their beauty, even during the storms of winter. Instantly, I thanked God for them and the lesson they had taught me about the importance of being consistent in the storms of life.

The list of possible faith builders is long. Books, especially biographies of dynamic people who have risen above affliction, can be a positive influence, inspiring us to new goals. Even decorative objects containing gems of positive truth may be used to spur faith to greater heights.

My friend, Richard Neale, the founder and director of Youth Gospel Crusade in Westboro, Wisconsin, sends out cards monthly that have encouraging messages on them. The one that arrived recently says: "*The Lord will either calm your storm, or allow it to rage while He calms you."* This one will find its place in a prominent spot in my study along with others he has sent, and I'm sure will be just what I need on some stormy day in the future.

Finally, expect God to minister to you through others. Remember that the Holy Spirit lives within each member of the family of God with whom you will come in contact today. Our Lord may have a message of faith to communicate to you through one of His children.

Many have ministered to me who were totally unaware of it. Often one has shared some simple truth or special experience without knowing that I was in need of encouragement at that very moment.

A widow told me of God's provision of money to meet a large need. That day I was also in need of a substantial amount. She knew nothing of my need either before or after her rejoicing, but I quietly thanked God for sending her across my path with her story of His faithfulness.

This kind of experience has been mine again and again since I have become alert to what God may want to say to me through others. But I have had to learn to listen. While I have an obligation to be God's instrument to enrich those I meet, I cannot expect to be helped by others if I do all the talking. Ministering to one another is a two-way street. In order to be recharged in faith through others, we must be willing to allow the blessings to flow in both directions.

Reprogramming is simple: *Reduce Negative Intake and Increase Positive Input.*

In computer language, the old principle still holds true: *Garbage In—Garbage Out!*

You cannot keep taking in negatives and stay positive.

A few simple lifestyle changes can make all the difference. But even these can be difficult to master when they require breaking old habits and, on occasion, ending old associations. Nevertheless, life is too precious to spend it in the pits. A whole new world awaits those who learn to rise above their circumstances and live each moment to the fullest.

4

No Time for the Pits

"How many hours do you expect to spend fighting during your life together?" I asked the prospective bride and groom sitting across the desk from me.

Surprised, they laughed.

Not many who plan for marriage talk about the time they may lose in coming battles. Perhaps if they did there would be fewer breakups.

A young wife and member of a couple's class that I was teaching told me, "My husband and I were just about to begin another argument when I remembered that fighting is a waste of time." She had learned the lesson well that I had taught a few weeks earlier and now was sharing how being conscious of the wise use of time had turned a potential conflict into peace.

A woman speaking to me on the phone blurted, "I'm disgusted with you."

"That's a terrible waste of time," I replied, kindly.

Yet some talk about the benefits of creative conflict between people who love one another. Nonsense. There isn't time.

My mother is one of the most positive people I have ever known. At eighty, she still sees the bright side of nearly every situation. She determines never to grumble or pout. "Life's too short," she says. And she has proved the power of that old adage to keep one living above the circumstances.

God's View of Time

Time frames are an important part of the Bible from Creation to the end. Without doubt, God could have spoken the entire universe into existence in a moment (Jer. 32:17), but He did not choose to do so. Instead, He took six days to do His creative work and rested on the seventh. During Creation, He arranged for the planets to move in their orderly courses so that man would have to reckon with time.

He created Adam and Eve full grown. It would have been well within God's power to have populated the entire planet then and there with mature adults, but He ordained birth, growth, and maturity, taking place over a period of time.

In the early years after Creation, God allowed people to live nearly a millennium. Adam lived 930 years (Gen. 5:5) and Methuselah, the oldest of all, died at 969 (Gen. 5:27).

Presumably because longevity amplified man's bent to wickedness, his lifespan began to shrink following the Flood. Since our time on earth has been drastically abbreviated, we ought to make the most of every moment given to us.

Time's great value is stressed in a number of Bible texts but the Psalmist David seems to have been most conscious of all the Old Testament writers about the need of using time wisely. He prayed, "Lord, make me to know mine end, and the measure of my days, what it is, that I may know how frail I am. Behold, Thou hast made my days as an handbreadth, and mine age is as nothing before Thee" (Ps. 39:4-5). He also saw the importance of investing time in quality pursuits and wrote that "a day in Thy courts is better than a thousand" (Ps. 84:10).

Again, the psalmist speaks of the eternal God and His view of time: "Lord, Thou has been our dwelling place in all generations. Before the mountains were brought forth, or ever Thou hadst formed the earth and the world, even from everlasting to everlasting, Thou art God. Thou turnest man to destruction, and sayest, 'Return, ye children of men.' For a thousand years in Thy sight are but as yesterday when it is past, and as a watch in the night" (Ps. 90:1-4).

To emphasize the contrast between frail man and his eternal God, our lives are compared then to grass that grows up quickly and is soon cut down, or to a tale that is told. It is noteworthy here that the lifespan of man is said to be approximately seventy or eighty years, just as it is today: "The days of our years are threescore years and ten [70 years], and if by reason of strength they be fourscore years [80 years], yet is their strength labor and sorrow, for it is soon cut off and we fly away" (Ps. 90:10).

In view of this continuing countdown, the psalmist prays, "So teach us to number our days, that we may apply our hearts to wisdom" (Ps. 90:12). Then he adds a prayer for positive living so that his life will be meaningful and happy: "O satisfy us early with Thy mercy, that we may rejoice and be glad all our days" (Ps. 90:14).

New Testament writers also give great attention to time. James stresses the brevity of life by comparing its length to a "vapor that appeareth for a little time, and then vanisheth away" (James 4:14). Peter points out the mystery of time by explaining that "one day is with the Lord as a thousand years, and a thousand years as one day" (2 Peter 3:8). Paul adds urgency to life by instructing his readers to redeem the time because the days are evil (Eph. 5:16).

Squandering Time

Time is priceless. A dying queen is said to have cried, "Millions in money for an inch of time!"

Each of us is allotted a certain amount of time. With a good amount of that time already spent, we then face a searching question: "How shall I use the time that remains?"

How do you want to use it?

How many of your remaining hours do you wish to spend in a negative, critical, or depressed mood?

Is that a needless question?

Perhaps not.

You may secretly, even subconsciously, enjoy being down—or down on others. Maybe you thrive on self-pity. In *How to Win Over Depression*, Tim LaHaye indicts self-pity as the primary cause of depression and insists it is a serious sin. He writes:

> When stripped of its false facade of excuse making and self-justifica-
> tion, self-pity stands naked and exposed as mental attitude sin. Those
> who would be most hesitant to commit an overt act of sin such as

adultery or fornication seem to have no compunction against this mental sin.[1]

Have you chosen to spend vital life time in a negative frame of mind because it makes you the center of attention and enables you to manipulate others? After all, "The wheel that squeaks the loudest gets the grease" causes concerned people to respond to your groanings.

Misery loves company so you may be among those who have found that your negative attitude attracts many who feel as you do. Those who specialize in seeing clouds continually enjoy gathering for your pity parties.

And perhaps since you are an expert faultfinder and an authority on everything that is wrong in your church, the community, and the nation, other downers know that you will furnish them plenty of moaning material. After a meeting with you, they will have griping causes for weeks to come.

Unwillingness to get involved in meaningful Christian service can be another reason for choosing to live negatively. I am convinced that much of the conflict that exists in churches falls into this category. Negative people would rather raise objections than give of themselves to carry out worthwhile projects; they would rather sob than serve. It is always easier to be part of a faction than to get into the action.

Relatively few, of course, desire to waste their lives in useless negatives. Forgetting time's relentless march, they have simply become victims instead of victors. In the words of the old spiritual song, they are "sometimes up and sometimes down."

Does this describe you?

Do you ride a roller coaster of delight and despair?

If so, facing time's fast flight may provide the incentive for change that you need. By following four simple steps you may find yourself out of the valley to stay:

Using Time Wisely

• *First, determine that you do not have time to be negative.* Decide to throw off negativism, depression, and despair, believing that you can do so.

Sound too easy?

Listen to Jesus: "Let not your heart be troubled; ye believe in God, believe also in Me. . . . Peace I leave with you, My peace I give unto you, not as the world giveth, give I unto you. Let not your heart be troubled, neither let it be afraid" (John 14:1, 27).

Our Lord is saying that we have the power to do something about our troubled hearts, our fears, our depression, our negativism. In his book, *Secrets of the Spirit,* Ray C. Stedman shares what this discovery meant to him, writing:

> At a time when I was experiencing a period of this kind of heart trouble myself—distress of heart—I thought of these words, and they came home to me with tremendously new significance. I saw something in that simple phrase, *"Let not your hearts be troubled,"* which I had never seen before. What impressed me were the words, "Let not." They mean that these disciples could do something about their problem. They held in their own hands the key to their release from heart trouble. It was possible for them either to let it happen, or not to let it happen. Our Lord is saying this to all of us; there is a way out of heart difficulty—this distress and fear concerning both death and life.[2]

The fact that we have the ability to reject negativism may come as a surprise to some who have been seeking a deep spiritual secret that would keep them from getting down, but our Lord's words are clear: "Let not your heart be troubled." We will do well then to accept the responsibility of our moods and actions and determine to correct them.

One brief statement by author Craig Massey in his article, "Pulling through Depression," has had a continuing positive impact on my life. He says, "While it may be difficult to admit, depression is a deliberate choice."[3]

Undoubtedly, there are some exceptions to Massey's conclusion. Moods can be triggered by physical conditions or mental illnesses, and in these cases there may be more than a decision to be depressed. Nevertheless, Massey's statement has been dynamite for me. The thought that I have at some time decided to be depressed assures me that I can decide to come out of that same depression. Finding myself in the pits, I can quickly think back to the experience that caused me to feel negative and deal with it openly.

"Oh," I say to myself, "I see you've decided to let this get you down." Simply recognizing where I am and why is usually enough to make me chuckle, and by then I am on the road to positive, productive living again.

• *Second, be thankful for the good things that are happening to you right now.* How many things can you name about your present experience that are true, honest, just, pure, lovely, or of good report? Thank God for them.

The moment you begin thanking God for His blessings, however small they may seem in your present frame of mind, you are on your way out of the pits.

Thanksgiving cancels negativism.

When I awake in the morning, knowing that my family members are well and have lived through the night, I can count enough blessings to keep me positive all day.

Most of us have times ahead in hospital rooms—or waiting rooms. If this is not one of those times, it is a time for thanksgiving, a time period to be filled with praise. If I do find myself afflicted or hospitalized on some future day, I can be thankful that my Lord has promised to be with me wherever I may be (Heb. 13:5-6).

Times of grief and periods of mourning await us all. It is appointed unto man to die (Heb. 9:27). In the future I will likely have to do business with undertakers and grave diggers. If this is not one of those days, it is time to be on top of the world. When one of those difficult days does arrive, I intend to face it with the promises given in the Bible for such heart wrenching occasions, but for now I will be thankful for life and the blessings that are mine today.

Jesus taught His disciples to pray for daily bread. If there is food on the table, it is a day for praise—not for pouting.

It often takes little to make us negative, but much to keep us positive.

Applying the first two verses of Psalm 103 each morning would break the chains of negativism for most of us, making us positive people: "Bless the Lord, O my soul, and all that is within me; bless His holy name. Bless the Lord, O my soul, and forget not all His benefits."

A woman going through difficulties told me she had been able to stay positive by practicing thought substitution. When a negative thought came to her, she substituted a positive one in its place. Rejecting negative thinking on a moment-to-moment basis, she filled her mind with thoughts that produced praise and thanksgiving instead of gloom and despair. Actually, she had chosen to use the Bible formula for peace of mind (Phil. 4:6-8) and her wise choice enabled her to stay positive in negative circumstances.

• *Third, seize each pleasant moment and squeeze out every ounce of joy it contains.* This good occasion will never return. There may be many other good times ahead but none quite like this one. Cherish it!

Ralph Waldo Emerson wrote:

> One of the illusions of life is that the present hour is not the critical decisive hour. Write it on your heart that every day is the best day of the year. He only is rich who owns the day, and no one owns the day who allows it to be invaded with worry, fret, and anxiety.[4]

The psalmist declared: "This is the day which the Lord hath made; we will rejoice and be glad in it" (Ps. 118:24). Lowell Thomas found such inspiration from this verse that he had it framed and placed on the wall of his broadcasting studio so that he could read it often.[5]

Jeremy Taylor said, "This day only is ours; we are dead to yesterday, and we are not born to the morrow. He, therefore, that enjoys the present, if it be good, enjoys as much as possible."[6]

John H. Vincent had the custom of repeating the following powerful covenant each morning: "I will this day try to live a simple, sincere, and serene life; repelling promptly every thought of discontent, impurity, and self-seeking; cultivating cheerfulness, magnanimity, charity, and the habit of holy silence; exercising economy in expenditure, carefulness in conversation, diligence in appointed service, fidelity to every trust and a childlike faith in God."[7]

Drink deeply from the present. Look for beauty that surrounds you but that you have been too busy or preoccupied to see. Listen for sounds that you have been missing. Hold someone you love and be glad that you are alive. Often I hold my wife in my arms and say, "I have right now with you."

In *How to Win over Worry,* John Edmund Haggai says: "Give every moment your all. Give your entire attention to the work at hand, the person with whom you are talking or dealing. The Lord grants unto us time only in the quantity that we can use it—one moment at a time."[8]

John Ruskin kept a piece of stone on his desk containing just one word: "Today."[9]

Think of the time you have left in life as money in the bank. Each moment the balance is reduced, and you are the spender.

Are you spending your money wisely?

Are you as wise about spending moments as you are about spending money?

A man who had just discovered he had a terminal illness shared his feelings about life with me. "It's been deceiving," he said. He had spent his whole life in getting and now had little time left to enjoy or use his wealth. There was no way to call back the years. The real purpose of life had eluded him.

Jesus told the parable of the prodigal son who received his inheritance from his father and then wasted it in the far country through riotous living (Luke 15:11-32). Finally, out of funds and friends, he found himself feeding swine to survive and feeling hungry enough to eat with the pigs.

At this point, the prodigal came to himself and decided to return to his father to seek forgiveness and to see if he could be taken on as a hired man. Upon his ragged return, however, his father welcomed and forgave him, placing a robe over his rags and a gold ring on his finger. Even the forgiving father could not restore the time that was lost in the far country, but together they could make the future better than the past.

Most of us have been prodigals. We have spent foolishly a possession that is far more valuable than money. Time has slipped through our fingers, and we have little to show for it. We have wasted precious hours being moody, negative, critical, gloomy, and depressed.

It is time to return to our Father.

He will not restore the hours that have been wasted. Those segments of time are lost forever. But He will make the hours that remain worth living if we allow Him to do so.

Time's Eternal Value

Finally, remember that each moment of time has eternal value. Believers are stewards of seconds. Each tick of the clock contains opportunities for Christian service in which we can lay up eternal rewards.

Successful business people realize that time is money. When Charles M. Schwab was president of Bethlehem Steel, he confronted Ivy Lee, a management consultant, with an unusual challenge: "Show me a way to get more things done, and if it works I'll pay anything within reason," he said.

Lee handed Schwab a piece of paper, telling him to write down the things he had to do the next day. Schwab did it. "Now number those items in the order of their real importance," he said. Schwab did that. "The first thing tomorrow morning," Lee added, "start working on number one, and stay with it until it is completed. Then proceed to number two, and don't go any further until it is completed. Then proceed to number three, and so on. If you can't complete everything on schedule, don't worry. At least you will have taken care of the most important things before getting distracted by items of lesser consequence.

"The secret is to do this daily," continued Lee. "Evaluate the relative importance of the things you have to get done . . . establish priorities . . . record your plan of action . . . and stick to it. Do this every working day. After you have convinced yourself of the value of this system, have your men try it. Test it as long as you like. Then send me a check for whatever you think the idea is worth."

In a few weeks, Schwab sent Ivy Lee a check for $25,000. This successful business leader saw the wise use of time as the most valuable ingredient in making his business a success, and he was willing to pay well for an idea that enabled him and his staff to accomplish more through it.[10]

We have a greater incentive.

The most underrated rewards in the universe must be those that will be given to the faithful at our Lord's return: "And, behold, I come quickly; and My reward is with Me, to give every man according as his work shall be" (Rev. 22:12). Still, most of us spend our time accumulating possessions that will not endure. Paul called this poor trade-off choosing corruptible things: "And every man that striveth for the mastery is temperate in all things. Now they do it to obtain a corruptible crown, but we an incorruptible" (1 Cor. 9:25).

The astronomical salaries of top athletes and entertainers are examples of how we have come to value time. People become wealthy overnight because of special talents or abilities. Their earnings in a few years will exceed lifetime incomes of most of us who work in other fields. But these big dollars are corruptible—temporary, as are the earthbound things they can buy.

Believers who earn big money have the responsibility of using it wisely for the glory of God, and if they do so can convert it to lasting treasure. But the exchange rate is far different than most imagine. On heaven's scale, the widow's mite amounted to more than the large gifts of the wealthy ones because she gave all she had (Luke 21:3). In the wise use of time, God certainly must also have his equalizer. We can all be good stewards of this valuable possession and will undoubtedly be rewarded in accordance with our talents, abilities, and opportunities. As we use time to its best advantage, we can lay up treasures that will remain.

Each moment has eternity in it.

Christians have the opportunity of investing their time in pursuits that pay greater dividends than any known on this earth. But a negative attitude can nullify these potential benefits by making Christian service ineffective.

Who will be moved to faith by one who acts faithlessly?

Who will be helped to understand God's love by one who acts as if God doesn't care?

It's Time to Be Joyful

A positive outlook is absolutely essential to effective Christian service. C.H. Spurgeon said: "You cannot glorify God better than by a calm and joyous life. Let the world know that you serve a good Master!"[11] And Spurgeon was but echoing the words of Nehemiah spoken long ago: "Neither be ye sorry, for the joy of the Lord is your strength" (Neh. 8:10).

Best of all, Christian joy is available. For believers, it is normal to be joyful—abnormal to be negative. In his book, *God's Cure for Anxious Care,* Dr. John R. Rice wrote:

What sin to leave the impression upon a sinning world that it is a thorny, troubled, defeated life to be a child of God! No, no, do not so dishonor your profession, and so slander the God you serve! Get victory over anxious care and be a happy, victorious Christian, shining forth like a joyful light in a sad and bitter and darkened world.[12]

Life is too short to waste any portion of it in the pits. There just isn't time.

5

Can't Afford the Money Blues

Never waste a day being down about money or the weather. If you can clear the clouds in these two common areas of aggravation, you will be well on your way to total positive living.

Rise each morning thanking God for clouds or sunshine, heat or cold, and you are sure to have a better day. Lift your heart in praise to God for His provision so far in life and your financial fears will likely fly away.

Rich People Fret about Money Too

Money concerns are common to all. And the love of money can be a danger to those of all financial positions, producing negative attitudes that manifest themselves in greed, bitterness, irritability, and depression (1 Tim. 6:10).

John D. Rockefeller, the wealthiest man of his time, pursued money with a passion. By the time he was thirty-three years of age, he had made his first million. At forty-three, he controlled the largest business on earth. At fifty-three, he was the only known billionaire in the world. In spite of having all that money, however, he was unhappy—because his money had him.

Once he shipped $40,000 worth of grain across Lake Erie without insurance because he thought the $150 premium was too high. That night a vicious storm raged over the lake, endangering his investment. Rockefeller was so concerned about his load of grain that when his partner, George Gardner, arrived at their office in the morning, he found John D. pacing the floor in anxiety.

Immediately, Gardner went out to buy insurance on the jeopardized cargo, if possible, while Rockefeller continued his pacing and fretting. Though successful in getting the grain insured, when Gardner returned to the office he found his partner in an even worse state of mind. A telegram had arrived announcing that the ship had arrived safely at its destination. Rockefeller was now so upset over having wasted the money on the unneeded insurance premium that he had to go home and spend the day in bed![1]

At the age of fifty-three and a billionaire, Rockefeller was described by writer Ida Tarbell as "the oldest man that I have ever seen." His health was so poor that he existed on crackers and milk. His hair, including his eyebrows and eyelashes, had all fallen out. Most thought he would not live another year. The money blues had nearly destroyed him.

Fortunately, Rockefeller recognized the destructive power that money exercised over him in time and began to take steps to free himself from its bondage. Instead of grasping for more dollars, he began giving them away, millions of them. He established the Rockefeller Foundation in order to channel huge amounts of money to worthwhile causes, giving large donations to schools, hospitals, research, and other projects to benefit people around the world.

The change from *getting* to *giving* worked a miracle in John D. Rockefeller's life. The tensions and inner struggles that he had known began to cease. In trading his self-seeking attitude for one of service to others, he became healthy and happy. By losing his life, he found it. The man who was thought to be near the end of his life at fifty-three lived to the ripe old age of ninety-eight and died having accomplished far more by his giving than could have been possible had he chosen to keep his wealth to himself.[2]

Most of us have trouble identifying with the money blues of a wealthy man like John D. Rockefeller. We chuckle at the thought of a millionaire pacing the floor and worrying about a cargo of grain when an insurance premium smaller than those we pay on our automobiles would have taken care of the risk. But we do understand the anxieties and pressures that money problems can create. We know all about the knotting up within that can come when bills are overdue, and we don't know how to raise the money to pay them.

Money Worries Endanger Health

Negative reactions to money concerns may be very human, but they can be destructive and costly. Becoming edgy over economic pressures can ruin your Christian testimony. Allowing resentment to build over money matters can produce physical and emotional damage and may bring about temper outbursts that hurt those who mean the most to us. Thankfully, believers do not have to be ruled by such emotions. Our Lord has provided promises and power to take us through the roughest financial storms.

In his widely circulated book, *None of These Diseases,* Dr. S.I. McMillan shares a personal experience about distress over money and tells how he conquered it. He explains:

> The stresses of living are not nearly as responsible for a host of debilitating diseases as are our faulty reactions to those stresses. The office of a physician is filled with people suffering from nearly every disease in the book because their minds are beset by a thousand worries about their finances, their health, or their children.
>
> Sometimes it is the doctor who suffers. Recently I was faced with a loss of some money. The loss was on my mind when I went to bed and it awakened me about 4 A.M. The next night I didn't sleep well because I was depressed. I am sure my adrenal and other glands were pumping an excess of deleterious hormones into my system. I think my worrying would have continued for a long time, but on the second morning I had immediate relief from my depressed feelings when I began to practice this verse from the Bible: "Be thankful whatever the circumstances may be." Before I read that verse I was the victim of circumstances; afterward I was the master of them.[3]

Reacting negatively does nothing to solve money problems. Worry will not put one slice of bread on the table nor delay the call of one bill collector. Blowing up at loved ones will not increase income. Arguing over bills at mealtime will build barriers in your home, but it will not prevent foreclosure. Irritability that affects your driving may cause you to act as if you own the road, but your horn blowing, screeching brakes, and loud shouting at other drivers will do nothing to slow the repossession of your car if you have not been making the payments.

Being Negative Is Expensive
Negative people compound their financial difficulties in a number of ways. Being down depletes energy and drive, affecting ability to work efficiently. When depressed, we are more likely to want to spend more time sleeping in order to escape our difficulties and this robs us of opportunities to increase productivity, which can often be the answer to our money problems. Solomon warned: "Yet a little sleep, a little slumber, a little folding of the hands to sleep: so shall thy poverty come as one that travelleth, and thy want as an armed man. . . . Love not sleep, lest thou come to poverty; open thine eyes, and thou shalt be satisfied with bread" (Prov. 6:10-11; 20:13).

A negative attitude is especially costly for those who work in positions that call for dealing with the public and who are directly dependent on customers for their income.

People buy more from positive, cheerful clerks, waiters, waitresses, and other service employees, and they return to buy again. Tips are higher to workers who brighten the lives of those they serve. Recently a sign in front of a fast-food restaurant read: "Help Wanted . . . Smiling Faces."

Even if those who meet the public are not paid through tips from customers, their income is more likely to increase when their employer's business prospers because of their positive contribution to a cheerful atmosphere.

Edgar A. Guest wrote:

> If I possessed a shop or store, I'd drive
>   the grouches off my floor!
> I'd never let some gloomy guy, offend the
>   folks who come to buy;
> I'd never keep a boy or clerk with mental
>   toothache at his work,
> Nor let a man who draws my pay, drive
>   customers of mine away.
> I'd treat the man who takes my time and

> spends a nickel or a dime
> With courtesy, and make him feel that I
>   was pleased to close the deal,
> Because tomorrow, who can tell? He may want
>   stuff I have to sell,
> And in that case, then glad he'll be to spend
>   his dollars all with me.
> The reason people pass one door to
>   patronize another store,
> Is not because the busier place has
>   better silks, or gloves, or lace,
> Or special prices, but it lies in pleasant
>   words and smiling eyes;
> The only difference, I believe, is in the
>   treatment folks receive.[4]

Positive people are also more likely to prosper because they dare to try new things. They venture out into untried fields, expecting to be successful. Sometimes, of course, they fail, but even then they rise up and try again. Often this spirit of adventure leads to financial gain.

Many who have been in dire economic need have given birth to ideas that have made them wealthy. Some look back with gratitude for tight times that led them into new areas or endeavors where they succeeded far beyond their former expectations.

Negative people draw back from adventure and risk. Their fears become reasons for noninvolvement and often even for laziness. Of such people, Solomon wrote: "The slothful man saith, There is a lion in the way; a lion is in the streets" (Prov. 26:13). This verse has become so practical in our home that we test ideas against it. Are there really good reasons for not moving ahead, or are we just allowing negativism to defeat us? Are we looking for "lions in the streets"? If so, we put the excuses aside and get on with positive living.

Since financial difficulties are a real and sometimes tragic part of life for great numbers of people, there are many helps available. Financial counseling services can be found in most cities, and some are funded by the government to make them affordable to the needy. Books on handling money can be bought in nearly all bookstores with several of them now published by Christian publishers so that there is a biblical dimension to their helpful messages. No matter which route one takes to get out of financial trouble, however, the old adage always holds true: "If your outgo is more than your income, there is no question about the outcome."

How to Get Out of Debt

Getting out of debt requires increasing income, decreasing expenses, or both. Increasing income may demand more productivity, a change of employment, or some bold new venture. We have already seen how important it is to be positive in these cases, but decreasing spending requires discipline. And a negative attitude shatters self-control.

When we are down, we are more vulnerable. In a depressed or bitter frame of mind, we are more likely to cater to our whims and wants, thinking this will relieve pressure.

A new suit or dress gives a feeling of temporary satisfaction.

Driving a new car imparts a certain sense of success, even when the buyer knows he has compounded his money problems with higher payments.

A few weeks away in some warm or exciting place seems like the perfect antidote for the money blues.

But these buying binges that promise relief often increase negative feelings when the bills start rolling in.

Now here's the good news: all the self-discipline that any Christian needs is readily available all the time. The Holy Spirit, who lives within, is more than a resident; He is a resource. He will provide self-control for every need: "But the fruit of the Spirit is love, joy, peace, longsuffering, gentleness, goodness, faith, meekness, temperance [self-control]: against such there is no law" (Gal. 5:22-23).

The indwelling Holy Spirit offers the discipline you need to keep from overspending. If you allow Him to have His way in your life, He will bring your wants under control: "Walk in the Spirit, and ye shall not fulfill the lust of the flesh" (Gal. 5:16).

If you do not have self-control, it is because the Spirit does not control you. And to be filled with the Spirit—to be under His control—is commanded for every Christian: "And be not drunk with wine, wherein is excess, but be filled with the Spirit" (Eph. 5:18).

To be filled with the Spirit is to be totally yielded to His will. Can you imagine being completely under God's control and still being controlled by negative thoughts with their unpleasant manifestations of criticism, bitterness, complaining, depression, and despair?

Impossible!

Spirit-filled people walk on higher ground. And the filling of the Holy Spirit is continually available to all believers.

While self-control comes from the Holy Spirit, negativism springs from other sources. James identifies them as follows: "But if you have bitter envying and strife in your hearts, glory not, and lie not against the truth. This wisdom descendeth not from above, but is earthly, sensual, devilish" (James 3:14-15).

Your money problems may have their roots in the attitude of your heart. By getting rid of bitterness, strife, envy, and other mental attitude sins, and turning the control of your life over to the Holy Spirit, you can live the disciplined life that is required to get out of debt and be free from the money blues.

Praying about Money Needs

Believing prayer will also be important in overcoming financial distress. Worrying about debts will not supply one penny toward ending your crisis, but God may choose to supply all of your needs because you have prayed in faith, expecting Him to answer your prayer.

My ministry began in a small rural pastorate. The church building had stood on that country corner for nearly eighty years, but it had never been used for a full-time ministry. I was to be the first fully supported pastor in the history of the church.

Taking the position there was an adventure in faith for me and my family as well as for the church. We agreed on a regular salary, and the people offered to supplement that with eggs, milk, produce, and meat as they were able.

When we accepted this call, we had two small children. By the time our fourth child was expected, the church had grown, and the salary had increased somewhat, but we still had no medical insurance and wondered how we would pay the hospital costs when the baby arrived. We prayed about the problem, remembering that God has invited us to ask and receive (Matt. 7:7-8).

For us, September 18, 1957 became an unforgettable day. When the mail came that morning, it contained a letter from a family in another community. I do not believe these people knew of our approaching expenses. Yet they had enclosed a gift that was within a few dollars of the need, saying they had sold their farm and that the Lord had impressed them to send this money to us. Our youngest daughter was born that night. Our mustard seed faith had been sufficient. God had supplied our need (Phil. 4:19). And right on time.

Eight years ago, I became convinced that it was God's will for me to conclude my pastoral work and enter a ministry of writing and speaking. I had been a pastor for more than twenty years and was at that time the pastor of a large suburban church. This change in ministry meant ending the adequate salary that I then received. For the first time in our married life, we would be without a regular paycheck. We had almost no savings, and this therefore was another adventure in faith for us.

There have been some tight times, but even these have been faith builders. Some of these experiences have brought special assurance of God's loving care, because the meeting of our needs has been so clearly miraculous that there could be no doubt as to the source of our supply.

When the electric motor on our water pump gave out, the repairman advised the replacement of both the pump and the motor. The cost was nearly $600. We had about half that amount, but that day a check came in the mail to cover the remainder of our need.

However, that is only half of the miracle.

Two years later, about midnight, we discovered we were out of water. I suspected the motor on the pump had gone out again, and when I told my wife she laughed. We were facing a number of large bills at that time, and one more didn't seem to make all that much difference. "What's five hundred more to God?" she said. Her positive sense of humor under pressure increased my faith, and I slept well that night.

Since I had to leave for a speaking engagement the next day, I called a pump repairman early in the morning. After inspecting our pump, he confirmed my midnight diagnosis and said the motor would have to be replaced again.

Dollar signs loomed.

Then, just before the repairman finished his work, a phone call came—*from the person who had sent the gift two years earlier on the day the pump had broken down.* The caller wanted to let us know that she had sensed that we had a special need and that a check would be delivered to our home that day.

When the check arrived, it was enough to care for our need. Our Lord's timely supply sent me on my way to speak at the Bible conference thrilled with His care and eager to share the encouraging message of faith with my hearers.

Fretting about money needs is always unprofitable because it demonstrates a lack of faith. Being down about the prospect of getting out of debt or being able to survive is a clear indication that no miraculous deliverance is expected.

God Provides

Actually, there are many examples of God's provision for His people given in the Bible, and in every case these miracles came when there seemed no human way out of the present difficulty. Indeed, if there had been another way out, the miracles would not have been needed.

When the Children of Israel ran out of food on their way from Egypt to Canaan, they were given manna, angel's food, that appeared each morning on the ground, with the exception of the morning of the Sabbath. The people were told to gather enough food for each day and on the day before the Sabbath, enough for two days. There was never any surplus good for food, but when the directions given were followed there was always enough for all (Ex. 16).

During a long famine in Israel, God sent the Prophet Elijah to the brook, Cherith, where ravens supplied him with food. Finally, when the brook dried up, God sent him to the home of a widow who had but a handful of meal and a small amount of oil left from the provisions that had carried her this far through the famine. She had intended to make one small cake for her son and herself, believing this would be their last meal. But in sharing her supposed last cake with Elijah, the widow found herself part of a miracle. Her meal and oil lasted as long as the famine was in the land so that she was never without daily bread (1 Kings 17).

Some Bible promises about meeting money needs are conditioned on our willingness to give. An example: "Give, and it shall be given unto you; good measure, pressed down, and shaken together, and running over, shall men give into your bosom. For with the same measure that ye mete withal it shall be measured to you again" (Luke 6:38). Other examples include Proverbs 11:24-25, Malachi 3:10, and even the often-quoted Philippians 4:19.

R.G. LeTourneau started giving when his business was near bankruptcy, and God in the years ahead began blessing him with great business success. Others have also taken this route out of financial difficulties and have frequently had their acts of generosity and faith rewarded with an abundant supply.

Money Tips to Keep the Blues Away

Consider a few important negatives that will contribute to a positive attitude when coming through money problems:

• Never talk about money during meals.
• Never talk about money when you are upset over other things.
• Never talk about money in bed.
• Never talk about your money problems immediately after praying about them.

Instead, follow this positive principle: tell your money problems to Jesus, expecting Him to pour ideas into your mind and strength into your body that will enable you to solve them.

There is no need for believers to have the money blues.

We can't afford them.

Being down about money indicates we doubt that God will answer our prayers.

Doubt impoverishes.

Positive faith rejoices in assurance of the Father's care. And that will always drive the money blues away!

6

Look for the Best in Others

When you feel down, consider if perhaps your negative feelings spring from disappointments in people, maybe even in people you love.

"Will you pray that God will take me home to heaven?" asked the depressed grandmother.

Upon hearing my refusal to pray as she had requested, this troubled woman poured out her story. She felt unloved and unwanted. Her son and his family, in whose home she lived, showed her little respect. Life didn't seem worth living anymore.

Perhaps you can identify with her.

Someone you trusted has let you down. One whom you have helped through tough times is not interested in returning the favor now that you are in need. Your employer has awarded your expected promotion to another. Your spouse has become cold and unaffectionate. Your children have rejected your teachings and become wayward in spite of your efforts to raise them right.

A well-known recording artist says she believes she might have been a spiritual casualty during the first year of her traveling work had it not been for the first three words of Hebrews 12:2: "Looking unto Jesus." Learning about the weaknesses and inconsistencies of numbers of Christians would have disillusioned her if she had not drawn strength from looking beyond their faults to her perfect Lord.

People Can Be Disappointing

Since the Bible is an inspired and accurate record of the lives of many people, it reveals the shortcomings of human nature. In reading it, we learn about how disappointing people can be to one another. In spite of revealing human frailty, however, the Bible tells of great strengths in imperfect people.

Abraham disappointed Sarah by telling the kings of Egypt that she was his sister in order to save his life (Gen. 12:13). But Abraham rebounded from this time of weakness and became known as the friend of God and the father of the faithful. Jacob disappointed his father, Isaac, by pretending to be his brother, Esau, so that he could receive the blessing of the firstborn son (Gen. 27). But later his name was changed from Jacob to Israel, meaning "Prince with God," and in his older years he lived up to his new name. Samson disappointed his parents and others by his unwise involvements with women (Jud. 14-16), but in his final hours he became a national hero who is named among the faithful in Hebrews 11, a chapter containing a biblical hall of fame. Mark disappointed Paul when he caved in under the pressure of his first missionary journey, but later Paul confirmed Mark's value as a servant of God by writing: "Only Luke is with me. Take Mark, and bring him with thee, for he is profitable to me for the ministry" (2 Tim. 4:11).

More than any other, Jesus felt the wounds of disappointment from those He loved. His brothers did not at first believe in Him (John 7:5). He did not do many mighty works in His home area because so few there believed (Matt. 13:53-58). Even after His perfect example of humility, two of His disciples, James and John, connived to get the highest places in His kingdom (Matt. 20:21). Though Jesus did nothing but good among His people, they tried to stone Him (John 10:31-32). Judas betrayed Him (Matt. 26:47-49). Peter denied Him three times (Matt. 26:69-74). Those for whom He had come to die, cursed and crucified Him (Matt. 27). Thomas could not summon faith enough to believe in the resurrection (John 20:24-25). Yet in all these heartbreaking experiences there is not one word of self-pity or bitterness from our Lord.

Why?

Because He understood the fallen nature of man and therefore was not shaken by its ugly manifestations. He had not come to condemn but to save. Beyond the cruel cross was the joy of bringing redeemed sinners to new life and this positive side of the cost of redemption made the suffering worth it all: "Looking unto Jesus the author and finisher of our faith, who for the joy that was set before Him endured the cross, despising the shame, and is set down at the right hand of the throne of God" (Heb. 12:2).

Many who had rejected Him would believe. James and John would become faithful apostles, preachers, and penmen who would turn others to eternal life. Peter would become the spokesman for the New Testament church, leading thousands to his Saviour. Thomas would believe after a week of doubt and would finally give his life as a martyr, being thrust through with a spear and suffering a wound somewhat like the one into which he had once demanded he thrust his hand in order to believe. These disappointing ones would become dynamic witnesses, turning the world upside down with their powerful preaching of the Gospel that had been entrusted to them.

Understanding the frailty of human character cuts down on disappointment when people do not come through as we think they should. But the key to staying positive is refusing to focus on the faults of those who fail us while continually looking for the best qualities they possess.

How Can You Say That, Paul?

Paul's letter to the Philippian church contains this startling statement: "I thank my God upon every remembrance of you" (Phil. 1:3).

How could Paul say this?

Was the church at Philippi perfect?

Absolutely not.

Churches are made up of imperfect people. At best, they are but sinners saved by grace. Therefore, no churches are perfect. Henry Ward Beecher said, "The church is not a gallery for the exhibition of eminent Christians but a school for the education of imperfect ones, a nursery for the care of weak ones, a hospital for the healing of those who need assiduous care."[1]

"I'm looking for a perfect church," a man once told C.H. Spurgeon.

"If you find one, don't join it or you'll spoil it," Spurgeon replied.

If the church at Philippi was not perfect, how could Paul be thankful every time he thought about the members there?

The answer is simple.

He determined to focus on the good things in the lives of the believers there rather than on their faults. This does not mean that he was blind to their needs. In this very letter to that church, he urged two women, Euodias and Syntyche, to be of the same mind (Phil. 4:2). These two were evidently at odds, but Paul did not allow this church problem to consume him or deter him from thinking positively about the church as a whole.

How to Ruin a Marriage

During my pastoral ministry, I thoroughly enjoyed officiating at weddings. To me, a Christian marriage is a wonderful occasion.

One of the tenderest times in the sequence of events leading to marriage is the first appointment with the minister. Two young lovers enter the pastor's study, hand in hand, with stars in their eyes, to find out whether or not their chosen date is open on the church calendar and to make arrangements with the minister for the wedding. For this important occasion, I had settled on a procedure that I felt would help the couple all through their married life.

First, I asked the prospective groom why he wanted to marry the girl. His answer was always essentially the same—because he loved her.

At that point, I wrote "He loves her" across the top of a sheet of paper while asking, "Why do you love her?"

An awkward period of silence usually followed that question. Often, I felt sorry for the embarrassed young lady whose future husband couldn't think of one reason to give the preacher for loving her.

One young man said, "Well, it's not because of her looks."

I've always wondered why we didn't lose that one.

Finally, after really thinking, a prospective groom would write several reasons for love.

After he had finished, I asked the same question of the intended bride. Since she had been allowed more time to think and had listened to the reasons given by her promised husband, she usually found it easier to list several reasons for her love for him.

Following this revealing time of questioning, I requested that the couple enlarge the lists we had started that day and that they bring them to our next appointment.

At our second meeting, I carefully went over both lists and returned them, urging both to keep them to refer to at any time they were needed during their married life.

"You are marrying an imperfect person," I warned, "and you both have faults that are still unknown to one another. After you are married, these will begin to show up, and when they do it will be time to go over your lists again."

What was I trying to do?

I was making an effort to teach the couple how to build a positive relationship. One of the best ways to do this is to avoid focusing on faults and build on one another's strong points. These positive traits were probably what had drawn them together and caused them to fall in love. I knew that if they started focusing on their negative characteristics, their marriage could be in danger of collapsing under the strain this would place upon it.

Ruining a marriage is easy.

All you have to do is accentuate the negative.

Those who build on faults should not be surprised when earthquakes come.

The same holds true for any relationship.

Continually thinking and talking about the weaknesses of the people involved will eventually destroy any marriage, business, church, or organization. But thinking and speaking positively about and to one another will make relationships strong.

Those Imperfect Early Christians

The early church is an excellent example of the value of conquering the negative thinking syndrome. After the resurrection, Jesus had commissioned His disciples to carry the Gospel to the whole world. This little group of followers was charged with the responsibility of evangelizing the entire planet. The task must have seemed impossible.

There were 120 believers gathered in the Upper Room following our Lord's ascension, and most of their leaders were proven failures.

If ever a group of people met together having the potential for disaster, it was that tiny band.

Peter had denied his Lord. Thomas had doubted the Resurrection. Philip had a reputation for expecting the least. James and John had tried to outrank the others. And the women present had gone to the tomb of Jesus on the third day after His crucifixion, carrying spices so that they could do the work of undertakers.

But ten days after this unlikely crowd assembled in the Upper Room to pray, they were the key movers in an evangelism explosion that rocked Jerusalem. Three thousand former doubters were added to the newborn church, and the world has never been the same since.

What changed potential failure to unparalleled success?

The answer to that question is found in Acts 1:14: "These all continued with *one accord* in prayer and supplication, with the women, and Mary the mother of Jesus, and with His brethren." Acts 2:1 emphasizes the unity of the group again: "And when the day of Pentecost was fully come, they were all with *one accord* in one place" (italics mine).

Somehow these imperfect people were able to believe the best about one another. They resisted the temptation to reopen old wounds. There was not one critical word among them. Putting aside their differences, they replaced Judas and prepared their hearts for the coming of the Holy Spirit, who was to empower them for the task at hand.

Many churches lack power today because they are given to quarreling, bickering, and backbiting. Like the Pharisees, their members specialize in nit-picking and are more concerned with revealing the faults of fellow members than meeting the needs of hurting people surrounding them.

Christian Cannibalism

In his letter to the Galatian Church, Paul accuses the believers there of Christian cannibalism, writing: "But if ye bite and devour one another, take heed that ye be not consumed one of another" (Gal. 5:15).

The Galatian Church had once been a center of dynamic Christianity. Love lived there. Paul said they had once loved him so much that they would have been willing to pluck out their eyes to give them to him, probably to improve his poor vision, if that had been possible.

Sadly, things changed. The church became legalistic and void of love. Now they gave their time to gossip and faultfinding. They had become Christian cannibals, eating away at one another, and their power was gone.

A pastor who had accepted the position of senior minister of a large well-known church said he found it interesting to watch certain members as they made their way to the doors following services. They were careful not to arrive there at the same time for fear of being obligated to shake hands or exchange greetings. Old grudges were deep-seated and the malice there would have destroyed the church had this ugly attitude continued.

What causes such carnal carrying on?

Focusing on the faults of others.

The Peacemakers

There is a high calling among believers that few seem to desire: peacemaking. A peacemaker cuts through the negative information that often floats around among Christians, dividing people who ought to love one another.

It is not easy to be a peacemaker because it goes against our nature. Peacemaking is contrary to carnal desire.

Yet Jesus said: "Blessed are the peacemakers" (Matt. 5:9).

What does a peacemaker do?

He forgets the gossip that he hears about others.

When the faults of his friends become the topic of discussion, he manuevers the conversation to another subject.

When he hears something negative about another, he doesn't feel it is his duty to report what was said.

When he is approached by one of two who are at odds, he refuses to allow his ear to become a dumping ground for criticism.

When he hears a complimentary comment concerning someone, he is eager to pass the good word along.

He is willing to mediate between those who are in disagreement.

He understands about the weaknesses of all people but doesn't major on them.

He has learned to bridle his tongue (James 1:26).

He is swift to hear, slow to speak, slow to wrath (James 1:19).

Peacemakers are positive people and are valuable because they turn the minds of those they meet from unproductive to productive thoughts. They help break down barriers and bind up wounds. They look for the best in people. No wonder our Lord said they would be called the children of God (Matt. 5:9).

Who's at Fault?

An unhappy woman thought there was no use in trying to save her marriage. Sitting across the desk from me, she told the reasons for her pessimism and unfolded a bitter story about her husband's faults. He was neglectful, unloving, mean, unspiritual, hard to tolerate in the home.

"Is there anything good about him?" I asked.

She hadn't thought about that in a long time. After a few moments of silence, she began to name a few redeeming qualities in this scoundrel, and before she left my office her whole attitude had changed. He wasn't so bad after all.

Looking for the best in others is not a denial of the sinfulness of all people. On the contrary, it recognizes the shortcomings in others and then acts in love.

Can you think of someone whom you have trouble liking? Is there one out there without whom you can get along nicely? Do you know somebody who can ruin your day by just showing up? Are you affected negatively by someone with whom you have to come in contact nearly every day?

Here's a disturbing possibility: *the fault may be in you.*

Expose your negative reactions to these powerful Bible commands: "Let all bitterness, and wrath, and anger, and clamor, and evil speaking be put away from you, with all malice; and be ye kind one to another, tenderhearted, forgiving one another, even as God for Christ's sake hath forgiven you" (Eph. 4:31-32).

This is the key to a positive outlook in our relationships with others: we must treat them as God has treated us.

Look inward for a moment.

What do you see?

Faults? Shortcomings? Tendencies to failure?

Probably.

Nevertheless, God loves you and has forgiven you because of your faith in Christ. "For by grace are ye saved through faith, and that not of yourselves; it is the gift of God, not of works, lest any man should boast" (Eph. 2:8-9).

And we should not stop there. The good news continues: "For we are His workmanship, created in Christ Jesus unto good works, which God hath before ordained that we should walk in them" (Eph. 2:10).

God has seen the potential in each of us and in spite of our weaknesses and tendencies to failure intends to develop us into what we ought to be. Having delivered us from our sins, He is at work, bringing out the best in us.

Shall we then think ill of others because they do not measure up to our expectations? Shall we target our criticism on those who have wronged us, being unwilling to recognize their value as individuals and reacting negatively to their very presence?

We have never been wronged to the degree that we have wronged God. Yet He has forgiven and works continually in our lives to enable us to reach our highest potential.

When we look for the best in others, we find them easier to love. And as we love those who are unlovely, we become more like our Saviour.

Another church joined ours in aiding a needy family whose husband and father had recently been released from jail. Together, we supplied food, clothing, and lodging for them. People in our church made attempts to find work for the unemployed head of the family so that they could get established and make their own way.

As time passed and little progress was made in moving them to self-sufficiency, I became discouraged with the project, doubting that this man was really putting forth much effort. I began to see our earnest efforts as a poor investment and voiced my concern to the pastor of the other church.

His response to my negative reaction has been unforgettable.

"It is better that they fail us than that we fail them," the pastor said. He was still looking for something good.

An anonymous writer in his brief but powerful piece, "My Eternal Preference," sums up the value of being positive about people, even those who may possibly disappoint us. He writes:

> When we are given our rewards, I would prefer to be found to have erred on the side of grace rather than judgment: to have loved too much rather than too little; to have forgiven the undeserving rather than refused forgiveness to that one who deserved it; to have fed a parasite rather than to have neglected one who was truly hungry; to have been taken advantage of rather than to have taken undue advantage; to have believed too much in my brothers rather than too little; having been wrong on the side of too much trust than too much cynicism; to have believed the best and been wrong, than to have believed the worst and been right.[2]

Caution: God Is at Work

The late Fred Renich, talented writer and speaker, added another dimension to looking for the best in others. "Trust the Holy Spirit in your brother," he said.

What an eye opener!

Even though my brother may not have arrived, the Holy Spirit is doing His work of sanctification in him, conforming him to the image of Christ. I can then look not only for good qualities in his character but for spiritual progress and positive change. He will be better tomorrow than today—and so will I!

7

Take the Long Look

John Wesley was walking with a friend who was defeated by problems that were facing him. Anxiety about the crisis he was going through had drained away all the joy of living. During their walk, they saw a cow looking over a stone wall.

"Do you know why that cow is looking over that stone wall," asked Wesley.

"No," replied the friend.

"Because she can't see through it," Wesley said. "And that is what you must do with your wall of trouble—look over it and avoid it."[1]

Trouble Doesn't Last

All trials are temporary, and we should look beyond them. Realizing this can enable us to stay positive in the most difficult of circumstances.

A king once asked his advisors to prepare a statement that would always be true. They settled on: "This too shall pass."

Peter stressed this comforting truth when writing to believers who were going through trials, telling them that their "heaviness" was only "for a season" (1 Peter 1:6) and assuring them that better days were ahead.

My work has placed me with people in the most trying times of their lives. I have been there when tears were flowing, when all the castles had tumbled, when the feared and unwanted had become reality. But I have watched these same people rise up after the storms and get on with positive living, often even seeing their former trials as learning experiences that contributed to later gains.

Businessmen who appeared to be on the brink of bankruptcy have prayed and worked their way to success.

Grieving people who had thought the sun would never shine for them because of losing loved ones in death have found God's grace sufficient and can smile again.

Parents who had nearly despaired over wayward children have hung on, kept the channels of communication open, prayed in faith and now rejoice in the good things that are happening in the lives of those they love.

Women whose marriages of many years had crumbled when their husbands had suddenly deserted them have been the most amazing of all in their ability to rebound and find purpose in life. There have been times when my heart has been broken along with those who tearfully told their stories of abandonment. But time and again I have seen the results of the power and comfort of God becoming operative in these tragic situations, and I now fully expect the deserted ones I meet to come through triumphantly.

Many marriages are restored that seem to have arrived at the point of no return. When I met Bill and Shirley Lyon, they had been divorced for about six months. Prior to their split, Bill had been drinking heavily, and Shirley just couldn't handle it. She spent more than two years coming to the decision to end her marriage. During that time she thought she had done everything possible to save her home. She had even tried attending church services, but somehow the church she had chosen did not meet her needs. Finally, she became a Jehovah's Witness. Three young sons multiplied the tragedy of this home breakup.

But the story does not end there.

Shirley's mother arranged for her daughter to meet with me so that I could share some things from the Bible with her. She agreed to these sessions only because she thought she might convert me to the teachings of her new religion, but following one of the sessions she was born again. A short time later, Bill also came to Christ. And before another six months had passed, Bill and Shirley were reunited in marriage. What had seemed to be an irreversible tragedy now was changed into a demonstration of the power of Jesus Christ to change lives and homes.[2]

Learning through Trials

Refuse to accept today's seeming disasters as final. Believe that God is at work and that in trusting Him good will come out of them.

At the age of seventeen, my friend Edward E. Powell, Jr. was involved in a serious automobile accident. He suffered injuries that required 137 stitches in his head and in addition to multiple cuts and bruises, he lost four front teeth. But there was another bruise that was more difficult to bear: a financial bruise. The car he had been driving was not insured and he found himself facing a debt of approximately $12,000. This was in 1951 when dollars had considerably more value than today and when wages were not nearly as high as they are now.

Concerned about his mountain of debt, Edward returned to work within two weeks after the accident. Soon he added a second job and asked for all the overtime he could get. Spending was cut to the bone. He learned to get by on bare necessities. Through hard work at two jobs and disciplined spending, he paid off the entire debt in less than three years.

Later, Edward Powell became an extremely successful building contractor and land developer, heading one of the largest building operations in this part of our state. He is now involved in a number of businesses and is an investment counselor. Interestingly, he views the automobile accident that took place in his youth as one of the key factors in his success. In his book, *Turning Points,* he says:

> I learned a number of lessons through this accident that might have taken many years to learn in the usual course of things. The pressure of that $12,000 obligation was a maturing force, teaching me that there are some debts we cannot escape. Being forced to face up to this responsibility made me a better man. I learned that one can face great obstacles and overcome them if he really applies himself.
>
> Facing that $12,000 debt at seventeen also settled me down. I had just begun to make good money and had started to live it up. But now

there was little money for anything other than paying off my obligation. While there were many places I would have liked to go and a
number of things I would have liked to do, I simply couldn't afford
them. I was learning the limits of life when one is in an economic
crunch.

Looking back, I can see that assuming this responsibility and de-
manding extra discipline and effort of myself was just the preparation
I would need for the huge responsibilities that would be mine in heading a large construction company later in life.[3]

For the disciples, there could not have been a darker hour than that
of our Lord's crucifixion. In preparing their hearts for that awful time,
Jesus said:

> Verily, verily, I say unto you, that ye shall weep and lament, but the
> world shall rejoice: and ye shall be sorrowful, but your sorrow shall be
> turned into joy. A woman when she is in travail hath sorrow, because
> her hour is come: but as soon as she is delivered of the child, she
> remembereth no more the anguish, for joy that a man is born into the
> world. And ye now therefore have sorrow; but I will see you again, and
> your heart shall rejoice, and your joy no man taketh from you (John
> 16:20-22).

The immediate future held many trials for these faithful men who
had left all to follow Christ, but after that awaited lasting joy and true
fulfillment. The best was yet to come.

The late Dr. John R. Rice wrote:

> Dear troubled child of God, believe me, the birds can sing for you
> again! God can give joy for mourning and beauty for ashes. He can
> restore the years that the locusts have eaten. The prodigal boy from
> the misery and want and heartbreak of the far country can again
> rejoice at the father's table. I tell you earnestly, as one who has had
> burdens and had them lifted, as one who is a sinner and has been
> forgiven, as one who has had many sorrows but found sweet comfort,
> as one who has worried and chafed and fretted and, thank God, who
> has learned to have peace.[4]

Needed: Telescopic Vision

We need to develop telescopic vision that enables us to look beyond
our present problems to the better things that lie ahead. Though we

do not know what tomorrow holds, we do know that all things in our lives are working together for our good and God's glory (Rom. 8:28). With this in mind, we can face the future with confidence, knowing that all the events of all our tomorrows are in His loving hands.

When Sue Latter was sixteen years of age, she became the Michigan high school girl's track champion in the 440- and 880-yard runs. To anyone that would have been a major accomplishment, but to Sue and her parents it was a miracle.

Sue's parents remember the corrective shoes she wore as a child and the constant threat of braces to help straighten their daughter's stubborn right foot. From the time she was a year old, that foot had turned in so badly it seemed as if she might never walk normally. After two years of treatment, braces still remained a strong possibility, but Sue's parents kept praying that God would heal her foot.

Imagine their satisfaction when a dozen years later, they watched their sixteen-year-old daughter win the championship at the Michigan state track meet in Lansing. Her parents were grateful beyond words, and Sue was also thankful for God's goodness to her.

Watching their year-old daughter struggle with her turned-in right foot had been discouraging for Fred and Katie Latter. Had they not believed in the power of prayer, they might have given up hope of her ever walking without difficulty. But faith enabled them to take the long look. And by the time she won the state championship, her running form was close to flawless.

Winning the Michigan state high school track championship was only the beginning for Sue. If her parents thought this was the fulfillment of their prayers and dreams, they had many pleasant surprises ahead. While a student at Michigan State University, Sue became an All-American runner. She has competed in meets in a number of other nations, and at this writing is considered one of the top contenders to run in the 1500-meter race for the American team in the 1984 Olympics. Sue is now married and is known to track fans as Sue Addison.

Her accomplishments in running have opened many opportunities for Sue to share her faith in Christ with others. This is a dimension to the answering of her parent's prayers that has gone beyond their expectations. Her father's reaction to how things turned out in the long run might well be a commentary on Sue's life: "God has given Sue more than we asked. We had prayed that her walk might be normal: now He's given us a champion."[5]

God often gives more than we expect (Eph. 3:20). Once when I was burdened about a problem, my negative feelings evidently showed in my face. Seeing my clouded countenance, a friend said, "Cheer up! Things aren't going to turn out as badly as you think they are."

What a rebuke that was for one who believes that God really cares! Yet, like me, many have fallen into the pits over pressing problems. If you are down today, you are not the first to be so defeated.

Pursued by wicked Queen Jezebel and her forces, Elijah the prophet concluded there was no longer any reason to live. He became so depressed that he prayed to die (1 Kings 19). But Elijah's future was brighter than he imagined. God would protect him from his pursuers, and he would be one of only two men ever to live on the earth who would escape physical death (2 Kings 2).

David was surrounded by foes who wanted to destroy him. Outnumbered, he might have given in to doubts and fears but his confidence in God's goodness sustained him. He wrote: "I had fainted, unless I had believed to see the goodness of the Lord in the land of the living" (Ps. 27:13). As difficult as his situation was, he was positive that God would bring good out of his present problems and this gave him the strength and patience he needed to survive—and keep singing.

The Best Is Yet to Come

In his comforting book *Dark Threads the Weaver Needs,* Herbert Lockyer shares a few experiences of that well-known positive Christian of the past, Billy Bray, the Cornish miner. Billy endured a great many persecutions for his faith but was never discouraged by them. He said that if his persecutors were to shut him up in a barrel he would shout "Glory!" through the bunghole. He had joy and comfort in spite of what happened because his happiness was not dependent on the happenings in his life but in spite of them.

Billy named one of his feet Glory and the other Hallelujah so that when he walked he would think of them expressing these words of praise. Lockyer points out that it was like Billy to name his feet and not the roads, for some of the roads might lead to gardens and others to gloom, but with him his feet still sounded their message no matter what the road said.[6]

This positive praising Christian miner is said to have prayed the following prayer each morning before going to the mines: "Lord, if any of us must be killed today, let it be me. Let not one of these men die, for they are not as happy as I am. If I die today, I shall go to heaven."

Billy Bray's assurance of heaven was evidently the key to his positive attitude. Every experience in his life was flavored by this unshakable faith in God's promises of heaven for those who believe. He had learned the value of taking the long look.

This was also the motivating force that kept early Christians victorious in the face of privations and persecutions. With the stones that would crush the life out of him already airborne, Stephen looked toward heaven and was allowed to see Jesus there awaiting his arrival. In light of this, he was able to pray for his executioners, knowing there was a part of him they could not harm and that their stones could only inflict pain for a short time, after which he would be with his Lord (Acts 7).

Christians are terrestrial transients, here but a few years and headed for a better place (Phil. 1:21-23). Paul explained that we make the journey from earth to heaven immediately on death and said that this hope should call forth absolute assurance and genuine anticipation: "We are confident, I say, and willing rather to be absent from the body, and to be present with the Lord" (2 Cor. 5:8).

Is the doctrine of heaven out of touch with today's complex world and unrelated to problems facing people in the troubled nuclear age?

Not at all.

Instead, it offers the only sure hope of better things to come. And hope is the ultimate object of trials that come to us: "And not only so, but we glory in tribulations also, knowing that tribulation worketh patience; and patience, experience; and experience, hope" (Rom. 5:3-4). Through trouble, we understand that God meets us in our need.

Do you fear that you will lose your home? You have a far better home in heaven. Jesus said: "In My Father's house are many mansions; if it were not so, I would have told you. I go to prepare a place for you. And if I go and prepare a place for you, I will come again, and receive you unto Myself, that where I am, there ye may be also" (John 14:2-3).

Are you suffering from some painful illness? These pains that plague and limit you will someday be forgotten, and the degree of your future joy will be so great that it will surpass any suffering you have ever known. Paul wrote: "For I reckon that the sufferings of this present time are not worthy to be compared with the glory which shall be revealed in us" (Rom. 8:18). And this body that now troubles you will be changed and glorified in the resurrection, never to be afflicted again: "It is sown in dishonor; it is raised in glory; it is sown in weakness; it is raised in power" (1 Cor. 15:43).

Have you been wronged by others? Snubbed? Talked about? Looked down upon because of your faith? Heaven will more than compensate for such trials. Jesus said: "Blessed are ye, when men shall hate you, and when they shall separate you from their company, and shall reproach you, and cast out your name as evil, for the Son of man's sake. Rejoice ye in that day, and leap for joy, for, behold, your reward is great in heaven" (Luke 6:22-23).

Have you lost a loved one in death? Do you hurt too much to face life? The long look will change that. Heaven will become more precious as you anticipate meeting your loved one there.

Are world conditions getting you down? Do you find it hard to be positive in this troubled world? Does the powder-keg condition of our planet keep you at the breaking point? Are you doubtful about survival? Remember that nothing has ever taken our Lord by surprise. The conditions of our day are prophesied in the Bible—even the concern of those who witness these things. Speaking of the end time, Jesus said: "And there shall be signs in the sun, and in the moon, and in the stars; and upon the earth distress of nations, with perplexity; the sea and the waves roaring; *men's hearts failing them for fear, and for looking after those things which are coming on the earth:* for the powers of heaven shall be shaken" (Luke 21:25-26, author's italics).

Do you often find yourself near tears because of problems you are facing? Heaven will care for those tears and they will never return: "And God shall wipe away all tears from their eyes; and there shall be no more death, neither sorrow, nor crying, neither shall there be any more pain, for the former things are passed away" (Rev. 21:4).

Do you feel that you have been cheated in life, receiving less than others? Have you become bitter because others have prospered while you have always had to struggle to exist? Our Lord will give lasting rewards to those who serve Him well: "And, behold, I come quickly; and My reward is with Me, to give every man according as his work shall be" (Rev. 22:12).

Are you tired of the money chase? Invest your wealth wisely, taking the long look. There is a way to make your money pay eternal dividends: "Lay up for yourselves treasures in heaven, where neither moth nor rust doth corrupt, and where thieves do not break through nor steal (Matt. 6:20). Giving is positive; greed is negative. Giving lifts you when depressed.

God does all things well and His plan is right on schedule. Often we do not understand what He is doing because our vision is so limited, so earthly. His ways are higher than our ways, and His thoughts are higher than our thoughts (Isa. 55:9). Resting in His love, however, allows us to see beyond our present trials. Faith expects better things ahead and accepts the fact that our present problems are but part of our Lord's training program for us, making more effective service possible.

Since our time on earth is limited, many of our rewards will come to us after this life is past. Heaven, the mansions, the resurrection, the kingdom, the new heaven, and new earth all await believers in the future. And in our wildest dreams we have not imagined what really lies ahead:

> But as it is written, "Eye hath not seen, nor ear heard, neither have entered into the heart of man, the things which God hath prepared for them that love Him" (1 Cor. 2:9). That in the ages to come He might show the exceeding riches of His grace in His kindness toward us through Christ Jesus (Eph. 2:7).

A man with whom I spoke had reached nearly ninety years. His clear witness for Christ was well known in the community where he lived, as was his consistent life. Our conversation turned to the subject of heaven. At the first mention of that promised place, tears came to his eyes, quickly spilling over their wrinkled barriers and washing down his weather-beaten face.

"The days are getting brighter all the time!" he said.

He had spent his life taking the long look and now he longed to move on to his reward.

My friend has long since entered his heavenly home.

When we meet again, I wonder what he'll say.

Since taking the long look will never be out of style in heaven, where joy keeps increasing as the future unfolds, he may just repeat what he said to me in that meeting long ago: "The days are getting brighter all the time!"

8

Don't Look Back

Satchel Paige, the famous baseball player, gained a national reputation for his rules for successful living. The best known of these was: "Don't look back. Something may be gaining on you."

There's a considerable amount of instruction in the Bible about the danger of looking back. Lot's wife looked back to Sodom during its destruction and was turned into a pillar of salt (Gen. 19:26). The Children of Israel looked back to Egypt, longing to return there because they doubted that God would bring them victoriously into the Promised Land, and it cost them forty years of wandering in the wilderness (Num. 14:28-35). Jesus said, "No man, having put his hand to the plow, and looking back, is fit for the kingdom of God" (Luke 9:62). Paul wrote, "Forgetting those things which are behind, and reaching forth unto those things which are before, I press toward the mark for the prize of the high calling of God in Christ Jesus" (Phil. 3:13-14).

Some Things to Remember

At the same time, there are a number of Bible texts that call for remembering, which is, in effect, looking back. While Lot's wife was judged for looking back at Sodom, Jesus commands those who live in the end time to look back to Lot's wife so that they can learn from her tragic backward gaze and be ready for His return (Luke 17:32).

79

Writing on the meaning of this prophetic warning, J.C. Ryle explained:

> A miracle was wrought to execute God's judgment on this guilty woman. The same almighty hand which first gave her life, took that life away in the twinkling of an eye. From living flesh and blood, she was turned into a pillar of salt.
>
> That was a fearful end for a soul to come to! To die at any time is a solemn thing. To die amidst kind friends and relations, to die calmly and quietly in one's bed, to die with the prayers of godly men still sounding in your ears, to die with a good hope through grace in the full assurance of salvation, leaning on the Lord Jesus, buoyed up by Gospel promises—to die even so, I say, is a serious business. But to die suddenly and in a moment, in the very act of sin, to die in full health and strength, to die by the direct interposition of an angry God—this is fearful indeed.[1]

Looking back to Mrs. Lot's destruction along with her treasures in Sodom is intended to promote holy living in the last days.

When instituting the Lord's Table, Jesus told His disciples to look back to the Cross. Luke writes: "And He took bread, and gave thanks, and brake it, and gave unto them, saying, This is My body which is given for you: this do in remembrance of Me. Likewise also the cup after supper, saying, This cup is the new testament in My blood which is shed for you" (Luke 22:19-20).

In looking back to the Cross, millions have found a powerful incentive for total surrender to God. Paul says taking this look lightly has caused sickness in some and death in others: "For this cause many are weak and sickly among you, and many sleep" (1 Cor. 11:30). Through the centuries, believers have met periodically to share the Lord's Table and in looking back to the cross have been moved to confess their sins and consecrate their lives to the Saviour.

Though Paul wrote "forgetting those things which are behind," he was quick to look back to his conversion experience and share the details of it whenever the opportunity came his way. Stand him before kings and governors and he would find a way to tell his conversion story. Clearly, then, he could not have meant that we are to forget everything that has ever happened to us.

The church at Ephesus had left its first love. Though feverishly engaged in Christian activity, this church had departed from the warm and wonderful relationship with Christ that it had once known. To restore the church to its first love, Jesus commanded the people there to look back to the time when they had loved the Lord fervently and had served Him with all their hearts: "Remember therefore from whence thou art fallen, and repent, and do the first works; or else I will come unto thee quickly, and will remove thy candlestick out of his place, except thou repent" (Rev. 2:5).

Some Things to Forget

So, there are times when looking back is proper and positive. But there are also events and experiences in the past that are best forgotten. When remembered, these have a negative effect on us, often bringing depression, guilt, and bitterness. In these cases, heeding just three words: "DON'T LOOK BACK!" can make the difference between staying positive and falling into a pit of despair. Here are some examples.

• *Don't look back at sins that have been forgiven.*

Forgiveness erases all guilt, assuring a clean slate for the future. It places the past behind us forever and turns away all accusing fingers.

A popular bumper sticker says: "CHRISTIANS AREN'T PERFECT . . . JUST FORGIVEN." And Christians really are forgiven. Consider the following guarantes of forgiveness upon placing faith in Christ:

In whom we have redemption through His blood, the forgiveness of sins, according to the riches of His grace (Eph. 1:7).

And be ye kind one to another, tenderhearted, forgiving one another, even as God for Christ's sake hath forgiven you (Eph. 4:32).

And you, being dead in your sins and the uncircumcision of your flesh, hath He quickened together with Him, having forgiven you all trespasses (Col. 2:13).

And from Jesus Christ, who is the faithful witness, and the first begotten of the dead, and the prince of the kings of the earth. Unto Him that loved us, and washed us from our sins in His own blood (Rev. 1:5).

In this day of big brotherism, complete forgiveness can be hard to grasp. Banks, the government, and many businesses have access to great numbers of facts about us all. Computers store information regarding every late payment, and difficulty in paying off a loan may haunt a prospective borrower for years, even though he has long since cleaned up the old account.

How different our Lord is!

Sins confessed are sins forgiven: "If we confess our sins, He is faithful and just to forgive us our sins, and to cleanse us from all unrighteousness" (1 John 1:9).

No cosmic computer contains any record against any child of God. All of our debts have been charged to our Saviour's account: "All we like sheep have gone astray; we have turned every one to his own way; and the Lord hath laid on Him the iniquity of us all" (Isa. 53:6).

I read the letter from a Christian woman in another state with great concern. She had been living with a time bomb for more than half a century. During that time, she had been respected and loved by her family and others and had lived an exemplary life. Probably no one suspected her inner turmoil. Nevertheless, the time bomb had been steadily ticking away.

In her youth, this woman had confessed a sin to the Lord and asked His forgiveness. That first confession became the father of scores of others, always concerning that same sin. Just before writing, she had become so burdened with guilt that it had brought her to the edge of despair. She was ready to do almost anything to feel forgiven.

What more could she do to be forgiven?

Nothing.

What more could she do to *feel* forgiven? Believe the promises of the Bible concerning forgiveness.

Like this troubled woman, many Christians do not dare to feel forgiven. Perhaps you are one of them. You do not doubt the ability of God to forgive others, but your case seems special. The magnitude of your sin looms large night and day. You confess the same sin again and again, yet it meets you when you awake in the morning and is often your final thought at night. You would give all you own to be able to go back and relive one regrettable hour. But that is impossible.

What can you do?

You can accept the fact of God's forgiveness. His love is greater than your sins, even the one that dogs your steps year in and year out. In doing so, you will subject your feelings to the fact of God's grace, as it is revealed in the Bible. Martin Luther said:

> Feelings come and feelings go;
> And feelings are deceiving.
> My warrant is the Word of God
> Naught else is worth believing.

The next time the bomb of guilt over some past forgiven sin starts ticking, disarm it with this daring declaration: "I have been forgiven!" Then refuse to look back anymore.

Discouraging Defeats

• *Don't look back at defeats that get you down.*

Only those who have never attempted tough tasks have escaped failure. And it is far better to try and end up failing than not to try at all.

After the death of Moses, Joshua became the leader of Israel. Upon assuming his position, he was given assurance of success. Though Joshua faced an awesome task, God told him that he would never be alone: "Have not I commanded thee? Be strong and of a good courage; be not afraid, neither be thou dismayed, for the Lord thy God is with thee whithersoever thou goest" (Josh. 1:9).

Things went well at first. The people accepted him. He led them into the Promised Land and mighty Jericho fell as he obeyed the Lord's command.

Then trouble came.

One of the Israelites, Achan by name, fell into sin. This robbed Joshua's army of its power, and they were defeated by the men of Ai. Not cowered by the news that Jericho had fallen, warriors from this small city chased Joshua's soldiers away, killing some of them.

Joshua was heartbroken. He tore his clothing and fell on his face before the ark of the Lord, staying there all day. All he could think of was the recent defeat. Never mind the flooded Jordan opening for his people to cross. Never mind the falling walls of Jericho, pushed down by God's mighty hand. All the victories were swallowed up by this one failure. And in focusing on his failure, he began to doubt his call from God, even that God had led them into this good land. He moaned: "O Lord God, wherefore hast Thou at all brought this people over Jordan, to deliver us into the hand of the Amorites, to destroy us? Would to God we had been content, and dwelt on the other side Jordan!" (Josh. 7:7)

But God would have none of this defeatism and said: "Get thee up; wherefore liest thou thus upon thy face?" (Josh. 7:10)

Sure, defeat had come, but there were many victories ahead. The new land must be possessed, and Joshua could not do that while groaning over the recent defeat. Imagine the negative impact on the morale of the Israelites had Joshua continued his crying and complaining instead of assuming his proper position of leadership so that they could get on the move again and conquer Ai.

A few years ago, I officiated at the funeral of a man who lived to his mid-nineties. He and his wife had maintained their home, keeping to some of their old habits to the concern of their children. They still did their cooking on an old wood stove and to make things more convenient for them, the children bought them an electric range. Months passed and the new range was not used. The old couple just preferred to cook on the wood stove. This meant, however, that wood must be brought in daily, and the anxious children urged their parents to make the change to electric cooking so that their father would not have to go out in the winter weather and carry in wood.

"We're afraid you'll fall," they said.

"If I fall, I'll get up again," he replied.

He had a proper positive attitude. And a biblical one. David wrote: "The steps of a good man are ordered by the Lord, and He delighteth in his way. Though he fall, he shall not be utterly cast down, for the Lord upholdeth him with his hand" (Ps. 37:23-24).

Solomon observed: "For a just man falleth seven times, and riseth up again" (Prov. 24:16).

This hardy farmer lived to a ripe old age while refusing to worry about falling and being determined not to keep looking back to his tumbles after they were past.

If you have failed, admit it. But never see yourself as a failure. Refuse to live in the past, surrounded by trophies of defeat.

• *Don't look back at decisions that cannot be changed.*

Some people live their lives in "if only" land. They are constantly second-guessing themselves, wondering if they might have chosen a better way in life.

We have already seen how the children of Israel kept falling into this trap. Arriving at the edge of the Promised Land, they sent spies to investigate it. Twelve went out and ten of these came back filled with fear. They admitted the land was all that God had said it would be, but they were afraid of the people who lived there. They saw themselves as "grasshoppers" in the sight of these powerful warriors.

Two of the spies, Joshua and Caleb, urged the people to move ahead and conquer the land, but their voices were drowned by the cries of the majority and the people were discouraged. In this negative mood, they cried: "Would God that we had died in the land of Egypt! or would God we had died in this wilderness! And wherefore hath the Lord brought us into this land, to fall by the sword, that our wives and our children should be a prey? Were it not better for us to return into Egypt?" (Num. 14:2-3)

Here are thousands of people intent on reversing an irreversible decision. When they were slaves in Egypt, they had longed to depart that troubled land, but now they think they may have made the wrong decision in leaving. Their next proposal is to appoint a captain who will lead them back into slavery.

Sounds foolish, but millions follow in their train.

Many live with regret because they feel they have missed the proper fork in the road. They wish they could go back and get a different education, enter a different field of employment, marry a different wife, or husband, move to a different area, or refuse to move to the one in which they now find themselves. They want a replay of history during which they can make adjustments.

Such wishful thinking is a waste of time.

We are where we are and had better make the best of it. Looking back will not change a thing and will only make us miserable. Besides, other decisions might have been more detrimental than those we made. Our present trials might be multiplied had we gone another way. The path we now covet might have led to disaster.

• *Don't look back at the past and see it better than it was.* Though their time in Egypt had found them under the whips of cruel taskmasters, the children of Israel cried, "It was well with us in Egypt" (Num. 11:18). At that moment they were hungry and their present privation added beauty to the past.

Memory can be like that—affected by our circumstances. When things are tough and times are hard, we may find ourselves looking back to former times and seeing only the positive things that happened then.

Distance lends enchantment.

Nostalgia is never quite honest.

Solomon warned: "Say not thou, What is the cause that the former days were better than these? for thou dost not inquire wisely concerning this" (Ecc. 7:10).

Some conclude that God is not able to work as well today as in the past. They despair of any great spiritual awakening in our time, believing the world is too wicked. They do not expect great answers to prayer because they have relegated all of God's wonders to history. They are positive about yesterday but negative today.

All such glorifying of the past is caused by looking back with blurred vision. Those who constantly look back to Utopian yesterdays become discontents today. Reality simply cannot compare with the dream world they have created.

Actually, yesterday wasn't that good, and today is probably not as bad as it seems. Dr. Vance Havner quipped: "The times never have been as good as they used to be."[2]

The important thing is to get on with positive faith-filled living for God today. This will make possible the building of a great future, which beats a great past every time.

• *Don't look back at old conflicts that make you bitter toward others.*

Here, especially, we must forget the things which are behind (Phil. 3:13). Most of us have had conflicts with other people. Personalities didn't mesh, strong opposing convictions wouldn't budge or somebody was just in a bad mood that day. Words have been said that wounded and looking back opens the wounds again.

There is so much in the Bible about being right with others. Jesus said, "If thou bring thy gift to the altar, and there rememberest that thy brother hath ought against thee; leave there thy gift before the altar, and go thy way; first be reconciled to thy brother, and then come and offer thy gift" (Matt. 5:23-24).

Peter says a wrong relationship with others will hinder Christian growth. He writes: "Wherefore laying aside all malice, and all guile, and hypocrisies, and envies, and all evil speakings, as newborn babes, desire the sincere milk of the word, that ye may grow thereby" (1 Peter 2:1-2).

Harmony among believers has always been precious. David wrote:

Behold, how good and how pleasant it is for brethren to dwell together in unity! It is like the precious ointment upon the head, that ran down upon the beard, even Aaron's beard: that went down to the skirts of his garments; as the dew of Hermon, and as the dew that descended upon the mountains of Zion: for there the Lord commanded the blessing, even life for evermore (Ps. 133).

But looking back to old conflicts can resurrect old enmities; even those that have supposedly been put away. Thinking through a bitter confrontation of the past can spoil a perfectly good day.

How many times have you caught yourself thinking about or even talking about all the details of an old battle that you had told the Lord you had laid to rest?

Just rehashing the differences and the things that were said is likely to raise your blood pressure and cause you to experience all the bad feelings of the former clash.

Are you at peace with some who were once your opponents? That relationship is from God. After explaining that bitterness and strife are sensual and devilish, James pointed out: "But the wisdom that is from above is first pure, then peaceable, gentle, and easy to be entreated, full of mercy and good fruits, without partiality, and without hypocrisy. And the fruit of righteousness is sown in peace of them that make peace" (James 3:17-18).

• *Don't look back at victories that make you feel you have arrived.*

Some who reach their goals make the mistake of not setting new ones and are content to coast through life from then on.

Pressing forward is positive.
Coasting is negative.
This is Paul's cry:

> Not as though I had already attained, either were already perfect; but I follow after, if that I may apprehend that for which also I am apprehended of Christ Jesus. Brethren, I count not myself to have apprehended: but this one thing I do, forgetting those things which are behind, and reaching forth unto those things which are before, I press toward the mark for the prize of the high calling of God in Christ Jesus (Phil. 3:12-14).

A.W. Tozer observed:

> One of the greatest foes of the Christian is religious complacency. The man who believes he has arrived will not go any farther; from his standpoint it would be foolish to do so.
> Religious complacency is encountered almost everywhere among Christians these days, and its presence is a sign and a prophecy. For every Christian will become at last what his desires have made him. We are all the sum total of our hungers. The great saints have all had thirsting hearts.[3]

Have you had some great victories? Are you tempted to relax because of them? Don't look back. There can be greater days ahead.

Are you getting older? Don't retire from the service of the Lord. You may have a greater impact for your Saviour than you have ever had before.

• *Don't look back to anything that robs you of Christian joy or hinders your service for Christ.*

• *Don't look back to anything that fosters a negative attitude.*

Keep looking up . . . up into the face of Jesus. He will keep you positive when other forces seek to pull you down.

9

The Secret of Contentment

Asked what he had learned from drifting about with his companions in life rafts for twenty-one days while lost in the Pacific Ocean, Captain Eddie Rickenbacker replied, "The biggest lesson I learned from that experience was that if you have all the fresh water you want to drink and all the food you want to eat, you ought never complain about anything."[1]

Still, many people with plenty of food and water, fine houses, and even large bank accounts complain and never seem to be satisfied. Strangely, a number of these negative people are Christians, having the Holy Spirit within, the promises of the Bible on which to rest their faith, a sure hope of heaven, and an assurance of the Lord's return to reward His children.

While Paul was never content with his spiritual attainments, he had learned the secret of contentment in daily living and thought it was so valuable that he shared it with Timothy, his son in the faith, writing: "But godliness with contentment is great gain. For we brought nothing into this world, and it is certain we can carry nothing out. And having food and raiment let us be therewith content" (1 Tim. 6:6-8).

Contentment Springs from Appreciation

Contentment comes from appreciating what we have, rather than longing for what we do not have. The Rev. Martin Blok, of Tucson,

Arizona tells of traveling through northern Michigan many years ago and giving a ride to a white-haired man who had been walking along the road. The two travelers had not talked long before discovering they were both preachers. The northwoods minister was at that time holding evangelistic meetings in a country schoolhouse, where he had been preaching for three weeks. His pay for his labor so far had totaled less than $2, but he was satisfied. The night before, he and his family had shared bread and milk for their dinner; it was all they had. His sons had at first complained, but he had reminded them that they had ought to be thankful.

"God has only promised us bread and water, and we have bread and milk," he had said.

His driver that day has never forgotten the lesson in contentment given by the aged evangelist who had so little but appreciated it so much.

In contrast, there has never been a generation of Christians on this earth that has had so much and appreciated it so little as the one living in America today. Angels who observe us must marvel at our quickness to complain when considering the privations and persecutions of believers in past centuries or in Communist lands. The disturbing dimension to this comparison is the thought that most present-day Christians might cave in if persecution came. If we are edgy in affluence, what might we do in oppression?

Paul said he had learned to be content at all times and under all circumstances.

How did he do this?

By the power of Christ. That is the context of the familiar "I can do all things through Christ which strengtheneth me" (Phil 4:13). While we usually apply this triumphant text to the accomplishing of some important task, it really has to do with being content in all situations. The two verses that precede it make this clear: "Not that I speak in respect of want, for I have learned, in whatsoever state I am, therewith to be content. I know both how to be abased, and I know how to abound. Everywhere and in all things I am instructed both to be full and to be hungry, both to abound and to suffer need" (Phil. 4:11-12). Yielding completely to Christ enables us to be content when others are complaining.

Paul's claim of contentment was not an empty boast. He lived a contented life in the most difficult of circumstances. When he and Silas were cast into prison after being beaten and having their feet placed in stocks, they prayed and sang praises. Their praying was not a surprise (most of us pray when in trouble), but songs of praise were not the usual midnight sounds in the prison at Philippi. This jailhouse doxology affected the other prisoners so deeply that when God answered the prayers of Paul and Silas by sending an earthquake that shook the doors off the prison, they all remained to hear what these two servants of God had to say.

Conditions were far from ideal in that prison. Tomorrow was uncertain and the present was painful. With their backs bruised and bleeding from the recent scourging and their feet locked in stocks, one might wonder how they could be content—even joyful. The answer undoubtedly lies in their use of the secret of contentment. They focused on what they had rather than on what they lacked. They were alive and were believers in Christ. Their sins had been forgiven and if this was to be their last night tomorrow would be better—they would be in heaven. They were not alone because the Lord was with them. The night was dark but Christ was their light. Weighing their assets, they found plenty to rejoice about and this moved them to sing praises to God (Acts 16:25).

You may also be in an unpleasant situation. You're tired of problems and feel whipped by recent happenings. Your emotional pain is as real as any physical discomfort you have ever experienced. How can you be content in this situation?

It isn't easy.

Sometimes things get so bad that all we can do is pray and wait for an earthquake. But while we're waiting for the ground to shake and the doors of our prison to fall off, we can inventory our blessings. The moment we do this, contentment will start moving in on us.

Contentment or Covetousness

Contentment is the opposite of covetousness.

Contentment is positive.

Covetousness is negative, sinful.

The fellowship of God with each of us can bring such contentment that covetousness can be overcome. The writer of Hebrews says: "Let your conversation be without covetousness; and be content with such things as ye have, for he hath said, I will never leave thee, nor forsake thee" (Heb. 13:5).

To covet is to focus on what we want rather than on what we have.

When the Israelites were conquering Canaan, the various tribes were given certain areas to develop as their inheritances. When the tribe of Joseph was given its portion of the land, the people were discontented. They thought their lot was too small and began to complain to Joshua about their grievance. Upon investigating, however, Joshua found that their lot was sufficient, but they were not willing to clear and develop it (Josh. 17:14-18).

Commenting on this text, Alan Redpath wrote:

> The children of Joseph were not satisfied with their lot; there was not enough scope for their gifts they thought; they wanted a larger sphere of service. Yet the fact of the matter was that in the sphere which God had given them the enemy was still deeply entrenched.
> Your complaint may be the same—that you do not have enough scope for your own abilities. Are you constantly discontented with your present lot? Do you often pine for a greater opportunity to serve the Lord? Is your heart set on some mission field? It may be that the searchlight of God's Word will disclose that the enemy is still deeply entrenched in your soul. May the Spirit of God point out to you that perhaps you have not really possessed the lot which God has given you.[2]

While the children of Joseph were coveting more land, they were neglecting the lot they had inherited. In focusing on their wants instead of their possessions, they became discontented. They were coveting instead of claiming, and so were not satisfied with what God had given them.

Those who do not cultivate contentment become covetous. In not appreciating what they have, they long for what they should not have.

Wicked king Ahab had many vineyards but began to covet the one that belonged to Naboth and offered to buy it from him. Naboth refused to sell his vineyard and the king was furious. Not content with his many holdings, he began to pout because he could not have Naboth's vineyard (1 Kings 21:1-4).

King Ahab's wife, Jezebel, found him depressed and, upon learning the reason for his negative mood, hatched a plot to destroy Naboth so that the king could have his vineyard. The wicked queen's plan was carried out. Naboth was falsely charged with blaspheming God and was stoned to death. After his death, Ahab took possession of the coveted vineyard. The death of a good man was the price of the king's lack of contentment and subsequent sinful coveting.

Covetousness is at the root of most crime. No wonder the Bible speaks out so strongly against it. Jesus said: "Take heed, and beware of covetousness, for a man's life consisteth not in the abundance of the things which he possesseth" (Luke 12:15). Paul ranked covetousness among the most serious of sins and warned: "But fornication, and all uncleanness, or covetousness, let it not be once named among you, as becometh saints" (Eph. 5:3). In his Epistle to the Colossians, he calls covetousness idolatry: "Mortify therefore your members which are upon the earth; fornication, uncleanness, inordinate affection, evil concupiscence, and covetousness, which is idolatry" (Col. 3:5).

Notice that covetousness is generally classed with sexual sin. This was, of course, its context in the Ten Commandments: "Thou shalt not covet thy neighbor's house, thou shalt not covet thy neighbor's wife, nor his manservant, nor his maidservant, nor his ox, nor his ass, nor anything that is thy neighbor's" (Ex. 20:17).

Some things never change.

King David's lack of contentment at home led to coveting the wife of Uriah while this good man was in battle. Soon the king and Bathsheba were involved in adultery and the infamous plot to get rid of Uriah and take his wife brought shame to the wayward king (2 Sam. 11).

The act is played out year after year and century after century. Husbands or wives stop appreciating one another and become discontented. They stop being grateful for what they have and start brooding over what they lack. Negative attitudes take over their minds. It is then but a step to lust and a broken marriage.

Contentment is a powerful force for good and the lack of it can be dangerous. Every area of life is affected by whether we are content or covetous.

So let's get down to basics.

Biblically speaking, contentment may relate to the bare necessities of life and the most difficult of circumstances.

Contentment with Food and Clothing

Paul advised Timothy to learn to be content with sufficient food and clothing: "And having food and raiment let us be therewith content" (1 Tim. 6:8).

I was born at the beginning of the Great Depression of the '30s. Those were tough times for the nation. Millions were out of work. Heads of families became desperate in their efforts to keep food on the table. Soup lines were common. Yet I knew nothing of these difficulties.

My parents lived on a farm where we raised much of our food, and though money was scarce, we were never hungry or without adequate clothing. My memories of that desperate decade are good. As a boy growing up during those hard times, I enjoyed a happy childhood. There was always food on the table, fun with the family, and fish in the creek. What more could a boy desire?

The world was in trouble, but I was not old enough to know or care. The basic ingredients of contentment: food, shelter, clothing, and love were mine; and I was blissfully unaware of the economic problems facing my parents and others in that tough period.

Life was less complicated there on the farm and people were then more independent of big utilities and big government. We had no electricity and were therefore never bothered by power failures. Our water was pumped from a well, so storms never affected our supply. Even my mother's washer had to be turned by hand to agitate the clothes, using up calories, and was always ready whether Edison was or not.

I was happy then because the basics were mine. True, I was only a child and maturity brings responsibility, placing more requirements upon us; but I wonder if our complex lifestyles are delivering what we need. This is not a call for everyone to return to rural living, but it may be time to think about the building blocks of real contentment.

Food and raiment are as vital to survival today as they were in Bible times. But are we as grateful for them now as people were then?

A meal delivers the same life-sustaining calories after being cooked in a microwave oven as over a wood fire in a cabin on the frontier. Strip away the frills of twentieth-century living and you still need the basics to live. We should be as grateful and content after finishing a meal in these affluent times as our pioneer parents were long ago. Actually, our source of supply is far more fragile than was theirs. Thousands go to bed hungry every night. When we have enough to eat and a shelter from the cold, our cups are running over. Too bad we don't recognize it! If we did, contentment would be ours.

Contentment with What We Have

The writer of the Book of Hebrews urges his readers to be content with "such things as ye have" (Heb. 13:5). Literally, this is a call to be free from the love of money and the pursuit of it.

The mad chase for riches makes negative people of many. Trying to match friends and neighbors in possessions has pushed many a marriage to the brink of disaster. It is so human to compete that few have the courage or wisdom to declare themselves out of the race.

As long as our cry for contentment can only be quieted by having as much as others we know, we will probably have many negative days. Christians may become especially frustrated when unbelievers prosper to a greater degree than the children of God. David struggled with this problem at one time and then shared the answer to it in Psalm 37, writing: "Fret not thyself because of evildoers, neither be thou envious against the workers of iniquity. For they shall soon be cut down like the grass, and wither as the green herb. Trust in the Lord and do good; so shalt thou dwell in the land, and verily thou shalt be fed" (Ps. 37:1-3).

It is not strange for unbelievers to become discontented when they cannot keep up with others, but for Christians it is totally inconsistent with their faith. Those who claim to love and serve the One who was born in a stable and had no place to lay His head during His ministry are completely out of character when they become negative over not having as many possessions as other people they know.

In many lands, families can carry all of their possessions on their backs. Here in America, most of us need a moving van. Floors of furniture and appliances grace our homes, and still we are not content. "Be content with such things as ye have" would be a good reminder to place on the walls of our houses. Appreciation for all the things God has given would be a major move toward contentment for the majority of us.

Contentment in All Circumstances

Paul said that he had learned to be content in all circumstances (Phil. 4:11-13). That's a difficult lesson to learn. Few have trouble being fairly content when everything is going well, but in this negative world we can find numerous reasons for becoming discouraged. We've already seen how Paul demonstrated his contentment under pressure in the jail at Philippi, but there were many other trials that put his claim of contentment to the test. Here are a few of them:

> Of the Jews five times received I forty stripes save one. Thrice was I beaten with rods, once was I stoned, thrice I suffered shipwreck, a night and a day I have been in the deep; in journeyings often, in perils of waters, in perils of robbers, in perils by mine own countrymen, in perils by the heathen, in perils in the city, in perils in the wilderness, in perils in the sea, in perils among false brethren; in weariness and painfulness, in watchings often, in hunger and thirst, in fastings often, in cold and nakedness. Beside those things that are without, that which cometh upon me daily, the care of all the churches (2 Cor. 11:24-28).

Can we be sure that Paul knew a deep peace and experienced contentment through all of these trials? Let him speak for himself: "I have learned in whatsoever state I am, therewith to be content" (Phil. 4:11).

Paul had a quiet heart in the face of suffering and death because of his absolute confidence that God was working out everything for his good: "And we know that all things work together for good to them that love God, to them who are the called according to His purpose" (Rom. 8:28).

Then let the storms come; let the key turn in the lock of the prison door; let the whip fall upon his back and false accusations be brought against him.

No matter.

Paul was persuaded that nothing could separate him from God's love (Rom. 8:35-39). This made it possible for him to use the secret of contentment in all circumstances. His appreciation of what he had in Christ was so great that his earthly problems seemed small. As a result, he was a contented man.

Constant contentment lies within the reach of every child of God. We have so much in Christ that no earthly lack can compare with our priceless possession. Keeping this in mind and remembering to appreciate God's care in providing the basics of life can bring contentment every day.

10

Health and Happiness

Sharp jabbing pains knifed into the left side of my chest, making it difficult to breathe. At first, I was not too concerned because I had suffered from these attacks periodically through most of my life, especially during times of stress or heavy exertion. And today had been particularly taxing.

In addition to caring for my usual duties as the pastor of a large suburban church, I had made a trip to Metropolitan Airport, about forty miles away, so that a friend could catch a plane to New York. I had helped with heavy baggage and then had fought my way back through bustling Detroit rush-hour traffic to get home for other responsibilities.

My discomfort had started about 11 o'clock, just as we were winding up the day. The pattern was familiar: pulsating pains in my chest, forbidding deep breathing. On other occasions, these had subsided within five to fifteen minutes, bringing great relief, but tonight was different. The pains persisted and after a time were accompanied by nausea. I decided I had better go to the hospital.

Upon arriving at the emergency room of the hospital, I was given a number of tests: X rays, electrocardiogram, etc. Finally, the examining physician explained that there was nothing wrong with my heart and that the pain had been caused by muscle spasms. He suspected that I had been working too hard and assured me that a shot of a muscle relaxer would take care of everything.

The shot certainly was relaxing. I slept most of the time for the next few days, had no more pain, and soon felt quite well again.

But I was not well.

The cause of my problem had not been treated, only the symptoms. And as the months passed, other symptoms began to appear. Many of these were related to nervousness, and this disturbed me. Staying calm became a battle. My cool was departing. Little problems seemed insurmountable. Irritations that I would normally have cared for with ease and forgotten bothered me for days after they appeared. At times tears burned my eyes, and the lump in my throat wouldn't go away.

Though I had considered myself an optimistic person, a cloud of depression now began to hover over me. I found myself speaking sharply to members of my family. Fears became my constant companions. Driving in heavy traffic began to bother me, and crowded buildings brought a feeling of panic.

Thankfully, my doctor correctly diagnosed my condition as hypoglycemia (low blood sugar) and advised a change in eating habits. Hypoglycemia is caused by too much insulin production which is triggered by sugar intake.

Up until this time, my life had been very sugar centered. My practice had been to start each morning with coffee, cereal, and toast. I sugared the coffee and cereal to my taste and spread the toast liberally with jelly. In midmorning, I had coffee and a glazed donut. When possible, I capped lunch with cookies or cake. Then during the afternoon, my sweet tooth demanded attention, and dinner was best rounded out with a piece of my favorite pie. Most any kind of pie is my favorite! Evening snacktime usually meant ice cream or some other dessert.

The diagnosis of low blood sugar demanded an end to my sugar spree. I had to stop eating desserts. But this was a small price to pay for feeling better. The muscle spasms that had plagued me for years ended, and my calm returned. Depression departed and fear subsided. Along with these benefits, a new appreciation of the importance of eating right impressed itself on my mind. I now saw the fallacy of thinking all problems of the emotions were spiritually related or caused by mental illness. Physical afflictions can make unwanted changes in our moods. Depression and negativism can have their roots in chemical imbalances or other problems in our bodies.

Lifestyle Affects Attitude

Though low blood sugar may not pose a problem, most people can feel better and stay in a more positive frame of mind by eating better and getting proper rest and exercise. Before my difficulty developed, I had made it a practice to work nearly the equivalent of two factory shifts each day. Often I sipped coffee late at night and in the early hours of the morning to stay awake and keep alert to study and prepare sermons. Now I realize I was pushing myself with caffeine and sugar beyond sensible limits. Finally, this affected my attitudes as well as my physical well-being. This had to stop.

My bout with anxiety and depression brought on by my low sugar condition has given me a greater understanding of those who come to me for spiritual counseling. I have learned to ask questions about the person's basic lifestyle and to urge him or her to consult a medical doctor to determine whether or not negative moods may be caused by physical problems. It has also taught me to ask questions about common-sense living that I once would have taken for granted.

Eating Right

The woman who stood before me had a fine Christian home. She attended an outstanding Bible teaching church and was at that time receiving counseling from a professional Christian psychologist. She wept as she poured out her burdens. Fears tormented her. Tears flowed frequently. She thought she was going to fail in a new project she had just undertaken.

Frankly, I wondered what I could say to her that was not being said by her counselor, her pastor, or her Christian family members. Then I asked her to tell me what she had eaten the day before our session. When she finished her description of nearly a full day of little but coffee and candy bars, I thought I knew what was wrong with her. After advising her to see a doctor to make sure there was not some physical problem troubling her, I suggested she start eating well-balanced meals. The next time I saw her she seemed greatly improved and in a short time was back enjoying life again.

David wrote: "I will praise Thee, for I am fearfully and wonderfully made; marvelous are Thy works; and that my soul knoweth right well" (Ps. 139:14). The intricacies of the human body boggle the mind. Though it has been studied by men for centuries and in our time tested and scanned by the latest medical equipment, it still refuses to reveal some of its secrets. Researchers spend millions of dollars annually trying to solve some of its riddles. One thing, however, has become more clear recently than had been supposed true in the past: the mental, emotional, spiritual, and physical parts of man are so closely associated that they affect one another.

Happiness Affects Health

Solomon pointed this out long ago, writing: "A merry heart doeth good like a medicine, but a broken spirit drieth the bones" (Prov. 17:22). Finally, we're discovering that the wise writer of Proverbs was right.

In his book, *There's a Lot More to Health than Not Being Sick,* Bruce Larson says: "Doctors have been telling me for years that 'you can't kill a happy man.' When I press for an explanation, they suggest that unhappiness often precedes an ilness. Happy people rarely get sick. The unhappy person is the target for any and every kind of sickness."[1]

If this is true, the Bible must be the most valuable medical book on earth. Its aim is not only to prepare us for heaven but to bring peace of mind and joyful living. In this negative world, God's Word is the source of positive truth that produces victorious living. Jesus said: "These things I have spoken unto you that in Me ye might have peace. In the world ye shall have tribulation, but be of good cheer; I have overcome the world" (John 16:33).

The miracles of the early books of the Bible inspire great faith. The Psalms stress the importance of rejoicing. The prophets dare to proclaim God's greatness and explain redemption. The Gospels announce the coming of the Saviour and describe scenes of healing and salvation. The epistles call for the filling of the Holy Spirit which is evidenced by love, joy, peace, longsuffering, gentleness, meekness, self-control, and faith. The Book of the Revelation unveils the kingdom, the King, and the new heaven and the new earth. Applying the truths of the Bible in daily living gives life a dynamic dimension that cannot be found anywhere else.

Once I asked a woman if she ever read the Bible. "Yes," she replied, "I read Psalm 91 every day." She had lived many years, and I thought if that psalm had served her that well it would be worthwhile for me to become better acquainted with it. Later, I discovered the reasons for her love of this rich Bible text. After giving multiple promises of blessing and protection, it ends with these words: "With long life will I satisfy him, and show him My salvation" (Ps. 91:16).

God Cares about Our Bodies

In my book, *Weight! A Better Way To Lose,* I show that God cares about our bodies. Consider this excerpt:

> God is interested in you. He loves you, all of you: body, soul, and spirit. (See 1 Thes. 5:23.) He is not like the hypocrite who claims to love a man's soul but can't stand the rest of him. It is true that your spiritual needs have priority. You are to seek first the kingdom of God and His righteousness (Matt. 6:33), but stopping there embraces only half the truth.
>
> Consider Creation.
>
> Everything in the universe, except the human frame, was simply spoken into existence. "And God said, Let the earth bring forth the living creature after its kind, cattle and creeping things, and beast of the earth after his kind, and it was so" (Gen. 1:24).
>
> Not so the body of man. "And God said, Let Us make man in Our image, after Our likeness; and let them have dominion over the fish of the sea, and over the fowl of the air, and over the cattle, and over all the earth, and over every creeping thing that creepeth upon the earth" (Gen. 1:26). "And the Lord God formed man of the dust of the ground, and breathed into his nostrils the breath of life; and man became a living soul" (Gen. 2:7).
>
> When Christ came to this planet, the human body became His vehicle of redemption. He was "made in the likeness of men" (Phil. 2:7). He referred to His body as His temple. He said the resurrection of His body would be the proof of His deity (John 2:18-22).
>
> The coming resurrection reveals divine regard for our bodies. Christ was resurrected bodily from the grave, just as we shall be at His coming. When that day arrives our bodies will be perfect without the aid of diets and doctors.
>
> Most encouraging to the Christian should be the fact that his/her

body is the temple of God. The Bible teaches that the Holy Spirit actually lives within every believer. "What? Know ye not that your body is the temple of the Holy Ghost which is in you, which ye have of God, and ye are not your own? For ye are bought with a price; therefore, glorify God in your body and in your spirit, which are God's" (1 Cor. 6:19-20).[2]

Since God is so concerned about our bodies, we ought to be also. We should be careful about keeping them in shape, guarding against obesity, as well as insufficient nutrition, and otherwise observing good health habits. These can have a positive emotional effect and contribute to better living.

Exercise Is Important

In addition to eating a good variety of food to have a well balanced diet and making sure we get adequate rest, we must get sufficient exercise. This may be the most neglected part of the average effort to maintain good health today.

In his book, *The New Aerobics,* Dr. Kenneth Cooper calls Americans the most inactive people in the world. We have grown weak because we have so many labor-saving devices to do our work for us. Our lifestyles cultivate softness. This often leads to obesity and a negative self-image.

Some Christians quote the Bible as a cop-out on any exercise program. Their favorite verse is 1 Timothy 4:8: "For bodily exercise profiteth little, but godliness is profitable unto all things, having promise of the life that now is, and of that which is to come."

At first reading, one might think that Paul was scorning physical exercise. A closer look at the verse, however, reveals that he was simply comparing the importance of physical exercise to that of spiritual. Naturally, spiritual gains are more important than physical, though in some cases they are closely related.

The Bible teaches, then, that there is value in physical exercise. It is not to be compared to such things as prayer and Bible study, but it has value, especially in maintaining good health.

My wife, as mentioned, has rheumatoid arthritis, a potentially crippling disease. We believe her regular exercise program has been an important factor in her lack of joint swelling and her ability to keep good movement in her body.

Once while vacationing in the Black Hills of South Dakota, we decided to go for a walk. Some of the terrain was quite rough, and she was unable to get up some of the hills without help from me and our children. That settled it. She determined to get in such good shape that she would never need help to get up hills again. Upon our arrival home, she started a regular program of calisthenics that she has continued through the years. Many times since, I have found myself hard pressed to keep up with her while cross-country skiing. Her exercise program has paid off.

During my years as a pastor, I regularly jogged from parking spots to appointments. This not only helped me keep in shape physically but also increased my efficiency, making better use of my time. Seeing a man run across a parking lot with a Bible in hand may have startled some. But if they concluded someone was dying, they were wrong. It was just someone living.

Benefits of Walking

Of course no one should launch into a vigorous exercise program without first seeing a doctor to be sure he or she is able to do so. But there are many types of exercise that are not at all strenuous and are still good for health. Walking may be the most valuable of these, and it is a natural tranquilizer. Often one can actually walk negative attitudes away.

Recently, I was surprised to discover how refreshed I was during the afternoon after taking a walk just before lunch. I had been fighting some 2 o'clock letdown and was having trouble concentrating at that time of day. It was a struggle to stay awake.

Walking changed that. A mile walk each day cleared my mind for the entire afternoon, allowing me to accomplish far more than if I had stayed at my desk and kept working away.

Weight loss is usually another positive gain from increased activity. Common sense tells us that burning up calories through exercise is a good way to control weight. And when most people maintain their chosen weight, they feel better about themselves. This positive feeling carries over into other areas of life and makes living more enjoyable.

We have a large lawn that we mow with a power mower. Because of its size, we've often been urged to get a riding mower, but we wouldn't think of it. Sometimes we divide the mowing so that we both get the benefit of the exercise, but on other occasions I get to do the whole yard. I can't tell you how many problems I've worked through or how many prayers I've offered while following that lawn mower, but I know these mowing times have always been positive experiences for me.

My book *Weight! A Better Way to Lose* gives more information on weight control and the benefits of an active life.

Living All Your Life
Changing your attitude about activity may even cause you to rethink your retirement years. In *There's a Lot More to Health than Not Being Sick,* Bruce Larson points out the fact that in the three societies sociologists have studied where people normally live to 100 and frequently up to 120, there is no special treatment for the aged. He writes:

> There are no retirement homes where people can spend their declining years playing shuffleboard. Scientists who have studied these three societies have found they have nothing in common in terms of climate, diet, geography, or lifestyle. But in all three places, the inhabitants are expected to live normal lives with no cushion of safety. They continue to work, tend fields, keep shops, and make love until they suddenly die at 100 plus.[3]

Some Christians use retirement benefits to support themselves on mission fields, but many more could be intensely involved in reaching their own communities for Christ. These people have wisely concluded that it is not God's plan for them simply to relax and wait for heaven's call. Many of them have become bored and unhappy and have decided to get busy about their Father's business, believing this will contribute to both health and happiness.

Recently, I ministered for part of a week in a church situated in a beautiful lake area of northern Michigan where more than half of the members were retired people. After getting acquainted, I began to see the great potential of this army of senior saints to do missionary work in the surrounding area. On the final night of the meetings, I challenged them to become so involved in carrying the Gospel to that community that they no longer thought of themselves as retirees but as full-time Christian workers. I am confident this kind of enlistment in the Lord's service by senior citizens everywhere would bring many who are now unreached to Christ and would drive clouds of gloom away for great numbers of retired people who are battling depression.

Good health and positive attitudes are then complimentary. Each contributes to the other. If you are fighting negative moods, you should probably see a doctor and have a thorough checkup. In my case, low blood sugar (hypoglycemia) was dragging me down, causing extreme fatigue, muscle spasms, weakness, depression, and other scary symptoms. Since many physical conditions can cause negative attitudes, it makes sense to get a complete physical examination periodically to see if some physical problem may be causing you to feel down, depressed, or bitter. Discovering that some bodily disorder is the reason for negativism can bring great relief and getting proper treatment can result in a whole new outlook on life.

One more thing should be said. While good health generally contributes to a positive attitude, many who suffer ill health are extremely positive people. They rise above their difficulties, being able to stay positive through their storms.

Like Paul, they find God's grace sufficient, learning that in their weakness they can draw on His strength (2 Cor. 12:9). They enrich the lives of those they meet and often comfort concerned people who go to comfort them.

God has given them songs in the night (Ps. 42:7-8). And their positive influence brings glory to the God they know and serve.

11

You're Dynamite

People have immense potential. We have but to look about us and see the developments of this age of technology to know that this is true. And the accumulated knowledge of the past centuries that has made these advances possible is only a tiny portion of all there is to know. We have barely scratched the surface.

Great Opportunities Ahead
The Prophet Daniel wrote of a coming knowledge explosion in the time preceding the Lord's return: "But thou, O Daniel, shut up the words, and seal the book, even to the time of the end; many shall run to and fro, and knowledge shall be increased" (Dan. 12:4). We can therefore expect continued progress and multiplied breakthroughs in all fields. The greatest inventions are yet to be born. The most potent disease fighters still await discovery. Space spectaculars are on the horizon that will boggle the mind. What an exciting time to be alive!

This is also a thrilling time to be a Christian. More tools are available to use in taking the Gospel of Christ to the world than ever before. Radio, television, and literature ministries provide opportunities for Christian service that are unparalleled in history. Local churches need committed people who will give themselves to reaching their own communities while there is time to do so. Make no mistake about it, God has something for you to do. But a negative attitude can keep you from reaching your full potential.

Moses struggled with just such a crippling problem. Though at one point he entertained thoughts of delivering his people from slavery, he failed in his initial attempt and gave up and fled the country. Then, after tending sheep in Midian for forty years, he returned to Egypt willing to settle for easing through life and minding his own business—but God had a better plan.

Not Me, Lord!

Speaking from a burning bush that was not consumed (Ex. 3:1-12), the Lord told Moses that He had seen the suffering of the Children of Israel and had heard their prayers. He then announced that He was going to deliver them from their Egyptian bondage and lead them into a good land, one that flowed with milk and honey. Moses must have been pleased with what he was hearing, but then the shocker came: he was to be the human instrument in this divine deliverance. The Lord said: "Come now therefore, and I will send thee unto Pharaoh, that thou mayest bring forth My people, the Children of Israel, out of Egypt."

Moses was stunned. "Who am I, that I should go unto Pharaoh, and that I should bring forth the children of Israel out of Egypt?" he asked.

Then he began to make excuses: "They will not believe me . . . I am not eloquent . . . I am slow of speech, and of a slow tongue."

The Lord gently assured Moses that He could make up for any human inadequacy, saying: "Now therefore go, and I will be with thy mouth, and teach thee what thou shalt say."

Still Moses protested and asked that someone else be sent on the mission.

Had Moses continued his negative thinking, he would have missed the opportunity of a lifetime. Focusing on his weaknesses and disregarding God's promise to compensate for them could have cost him the fulfilling of the purpose for which he had been born. Fortunately, he surrendered to the will of God and embarked on the greatest adventure of his life. As a result, he became a national hero and one of the key characters of the Old Testament.

His rank as a servant of God is shown by his appearance with Elijah on the Mount of Transfiguration (Matt. 17). And the last book in the

Bible reveals that he is the composer of one of heaven's songs: "And they sing the song of Moses the servant of God, and the song of the Lamb, saying, Great and marvelous are Thy works, Lord God Almighty; just and true are Thy ways, Thou King of saints" (Rev. 15:3).

Reasons for Noninvolvement

All of these achievements and rewards could have been lost there in the desert of Midian as Moses stood before the burning bush. His self-criticism and lack of faith that God could use him could have ruined everything. Though some may consider his excuse-making a sign of humility, it was instead a mark of negativism and unbelief. These excuses may have even had their roots in pride. He had attempted to deliver his people once before and had failed. Perhaps he was unwilling to risk embarrassment again.

A missionary told me that he had found it difficult to speak before crowds to tell of his work during the time he was raising support to go to the field. He would become nervous and ill-at-ease, dreading the responsibility. Then he realized his problem was pride. He feared doing a poor job in his presentation and was shrinking from a possible negative reaction by his listeners.

"When I discovered my problem was pride, I knew what God wanted me to do," he said. "I confessed it as sin and was rid of it at last."

My missionary friend is not the only one to fear public speaking. Some studies show this to the the number 1 fear among Americans. Even the Prophet Jeremiah faced it, and I have identified with him and read the first chapter of his prophecy hundreds of times while sitting on platforms awaiting my time to speak. Telling the story of his negative feelings about public speaking and God's answer to them, Jeremiah wrote:

Then said I, Ah, Lord God! behold, I cannot speak, for I am a child. But the Lord said unto me, Say not, I am a child, for thou shalt go to all that I shall send thee, and whatsoever I command thee, thou shalt speak. Be not afraid of their faces, for I am with thee to deliver thee saith the Lord. Then the Lord put forth His hand, and touched my mouth. And the Lord said unto me, Behold, I have put My words in thy mouth (Jer. 1:6-9).

God's Power Makes the Difference

Humanly speaking, Moses would have been unable to lead Israel out of Egypt, but going in God's power he could not fail. Whatever Jeremiah's public speaking ability may have been, he was up to the task assigned him because God touched his mouth and promised to fill it with His words. David certainly was no match for Goliath, but approaching the duel in divine power made him victorious.

One with God is a majority.

Henry Varley, a close friend of D.L. Moody in the early days of his ministry, said, "It remains to be seen what God will do with a man who gives himself up wholly to Him." Moody determined to be that man.[1] And while we are unable to measure the exact degree of another person's dedication, there is ample evidence that this shoe salesman without theological training accomplished great things in the power of God. The impact of his useful life is still felt by millions through the institutions he founded, and as a result of them his ministry continues to reach many for Christ to this day. Your similar surrender might open doors for you surpassing anything you have ever imagined.

You probably have had dreams of achieving success and recognition which have never materialized. Perhaps these had to do with your work, some other type of work you would like to be in, a hobby, or even an athletic achievement. They may have focused on some work for Christ to which you once felt called but for which you did not prepare nor dare to enter. Perhaps like Moses in Midian, you've shelved these goals, having resigned yourself to living in the desert of defeat. Your failure to seize opportunities and carry through on them is one of the causes of your negativism. Life has been disappointing and you have difficulty being positive about anything.

Get off that treadmill of bitterness.

You Can Do It!

Stop looking back at failures and start thinking big. Reject the low self-image that haunts you every time you are about to move ahead on some opportunity that has come your way.

Don't think about being a loser.

Tune out all the cutting negative voices of the past that have kept you from believing you are able to do worthwhile things. Some people spend their lives being imprisoned by caustic comments made by others in times of disgust or anger. Often these have long since been forgotten by those who made them. How sad to live a restricted life because someone in a bad mood vented his or her negativism on you!

Instead, remember the encouragements of yesterday and make them work for you today. Solomon wrote: "Heaviness in the heart of man maketh it stoop, but a good word maketh it glad" (Prov. 12:25). Remember the good words that made you glad.

When I was fifteen, my high school English teacher came to my desk one day and said, "I like the way you write." I was surprised at her comment and felt good about it.

Though I did not then decide to pursue a career in writing, there came a time several years later when I became interested in speak-ing out on a subject and wrote an article about it. While trying to work up enough courage to send the article to a magazine to see if it might be published, I remembered that teacher's encouraging words and I quickly gained enough confidence to mail it and risk possible rejection.

The article was published, and this built my confidence enough to write another. Upon publication, the second article was reprinted by a number of other magazines and was placed in booklet form by a well-known publisher. The amount of interest in this second article gave birth to my first book, which was a further study of the same subject.

I'm sure I have received my share of negative comments in life, but I have made it a point to forget them. That one encouraging state-ment by my English teacher was worth more than all the negative ones. Keep good words; throw the downers away.

The Prophet Jonah is an excellent example of one who failed and then came back to succeed. Called by God to warn wicked Nineveh of coming destruction, Jonah rebelled and tried to flee. Hurrying down to Joppa, he boarded a ship headed for Tarshish and went down into the lower part to sleep. While he slept, a severe storm arose and it appeared that the ship would come apart, taking the lives of all on board.

Awakened, Jonah told the sailors that he was the cause of their problem and advised them to throw him overboard. When they did this, the sea became calm. Jonah, however, was swallowed by a great fish that had been prepared by the Lord for this occasion (Jonah 1).

After his trying experience in the fish, Jonah was called again and given his original commission: he was to go to Nineveh and deliver God's message. When he did this, the entire city repented, causing the threat of judgment to be lifted (Jonah 3).

How strange.

Here is a man who rebelled and failed and yet became successful in turning an entire city to God, one that was so wicked that it had been marked for judgment. He worked alone, without media coverage or even a public address system, but 600,000 people repented within forty days. Here, God used a man who seemed poorly qualified and the city was spared from destruction. Like Jonah, many who have not measured up to man's standards have been effective servants of God.

By conventional standards, the disciples were poorly educated. In addition, they had conducted themselves badly during the trial and crucifixion of Jesus. Nevertheless, they shook Jerusalem and the surrounding area on the Day of Pentecost and after. There could be but one explanation: the Lord was with them. This, of course, had been the promise of the Great Commission: "And Jesus came and spake unto them, saying, All power is given unto Me in heaven and in earth. Go ye therefore, and teach all nations, baptizing them in the name of the Father, and of the Son, and of the Holy Ghost, teaching them to observe all things whatsoever I have commanded you: and, lo, I am with you alway, even unto the end of the world" (Matt. 28:18-20).

The people of that day recognized that God's power was working through the disciples. Consequently, their effectiveness in spite of their lack of learning became a confirmation of their relationship with the Lord. His power gave authority to their preaching. Luke describes what took place: "Now when they saw the boldness of Peter and John and perceived that they were unlearned and ignorant men, they marveled, and they took knowledge of them, that they had been with Jesus" (Acts 4:13).

The People God Uses

Do you feel inferior? Unqualified? Unlikely to be chosen by God for any significant task?

Consider Paul's explanation about the kinds of people God uses to accomplish His work: "But God hath chosen the foolish things of the world to confound the wise; and God hath chosen the weak things of the world to confound the things which are mighty; and base things of the world, and things which are despised, hath God chosen, yea, and things which are not, to bring to nought things that are, that no flesh should glory in His presence" (1 Cor. 1:27-29).

What kind of a man do you think Moses was? Dictatorial? Hard driving? The strong executive type?

Hardly.

Here is one description of him given in the Bible: "Now the man Moses was very meek, above all the men which were upon the face of the earth" (Num. 12:3). Yet he was chosen by the Lord for one of the most difficult tasks of history.

John Wesley was born in 1703 and his life spanned nearly an entire century. He died in 1791. He was God's man of the hour for England.

At the time of Wesley's birth, social and moral conditions in England were deplorable. Coarseness and brutality were common. The slave trade flourished with its violence and disregard for human worth. Smuggling and thievery were rampant, as was immorality. The lot of the working people was almost unbearable. Bread winners were imprisoned for debts. A laborer's life was one of drudgery under miserable working conditions. Young children slaved in mines and mills for up to 14 hours a day.

The religious life of England was not any better. Sermons in the churches had become little more than dry and colorless talks on morality. Most of the clergy seemed to care little for their congregations, being more interested in fox hunting, card playing, and drinking.

By the time of Wesley's death, however, the nation had been changed. The Wesleyan Revival had transformed England during John's lifetime, though he must have seemed an unlikely candidate to be chosen by God for such a mission. A small man, Wesley at only 120 pounds was not an imposing figure, and his plain speaking caused him to be shut out of most of the pulpits of the land. Nevertheless, he was the man God used, along with his brother Charles, to call the nation to repentance and genuine revival.

Billy Sunday was a professional baseball player who was converted at the Pacific Garden Mission in Chicago. He had no formal training for the ministry, but God's hand was clearly upon him in his ministry.

Sunday held great evangelistic crusades across the land. Huge tabernacles were built for his meetings in many cities. He met people where they were, spoke their language, and great numbers came to Christ.

Billy was unique. He was one of a kind. Fortunately, he did not allow this to stop him from serving the Lord. Being cut out of a different pattern than other ministers of his time simply increased his effectiveness. He was different, but he was dynamite and the entire nation felt the impact of his ministry.

But you're dynamite too—and unique!

You probably have talents that have not been used to their fullest potential—gifts that are going to waste. Energy flows through you each day that should be used for the glory of God and to enrich your life.

Special and Gifted

Your body is the temple of the Holy Spirit. In the words of A.W. Tozer, you are "the dwelling place of God."[2] As a believer in Christ, you are a partaker of the divine nature (2 Peter 2:4). You are equipped to win!

Since you are part of the body of Christ, you are flesh and bone of the living organism through which our Lord works in this world. Regardless of your natural ability or appearance, you are very special to God. No other Christian is more important to Him:

If the foot shall say, Because I am not the hand, I am not of the body; is it therefore not of the body? And if the ear shall say, Because I am not the eye, I am not of the body; is it therefore, not of the body? If the whole body were an eye, where were the hearing? If the whole were hearing, where were the smelling? But now hath God set the members, every one of them, in the body, as it hath pleased Him (1 Cor. 12:15-18).

Here's more good news: every believer has been given at least one gift to use in serving the Lord. Not one child of God can claim uselessness. These gifts make it possible for every one of us to be effective servants of God and helpful to others. Paul explained:

> For as we have many members in one body, and all members have not the same office, so we, being many are one body in Christ, and every one members of one another. Having gifts differing according to the grace that is given to us, whether prophecy, let us prophesy according to the proportion of faith; or ministry, let us wait on our ministering; or he that teacheth, on teaching, or he that exhorteth, on exhortation; he that giveth, let him do it with simplicity; he that ruleth, with diligence; he that showeth mercy, with cheerfulness (Rom. 12:4-8).

The major portions of the Bible that explain spiritual gifts are Romans 12, 1 Corinthians 12—14, and Ephesians 4. Remember, you possess at least one of the gifts mentioned in these powerful texts.

A friend of mine recently told me how encouraging it has been to him to discover he has the gift of *helps* (1 Cor. 12:28). He had not known that each believer has at least one gift and had not even been aware of the gift of *helps.* Though he has been helpful to many people in the past, he is now eagerly looking for more opportunities to use this gift to the glory of God.

If you have trouble discerning which gift or gifts you possess, start by following the advice of Leslie Flynn in his book, *19 Gifts of the Spirit* (Victor). He writes:

> Even if we thought we had no gifts, or were unaware of our responsibility to discover and develop our gifts, we do possess hundreds of New Testament commands which operate in the area of gifts. Everyone, without possessing the following gifts, is enjoined to evangelize, exhort, show mercy, and help. As we begin to obey in these or other spheres, the Holy Spirit gradually unveils certain gifts. So we should get busy in Christian service.[3]

For Such a Time as This

In addition to being empowered by the Holy Spirit and gifted to serve, we can expect our circumstances to be conducive to doing God's will. Great opportunities will come our way and we must be willing to seize them.

Esther was the queen of Persia at a time when her people, the Jews, were in great jeopardy. Haman, one of the top officials in the kingdom, had developed a strong hatred for them and had convinced the king to do away with all the Jews in the land. The king, Ahasuerus, did not know that Esther was a Jew.

In an effort to save his people, Esther's cousin, Mordecai, asked her to go to the king and intercede for them. Fearing for her life, she answered negatively: there was nothing she could do.

Then Mordecai challenged Esther with one of the most thought-provoking questions in the Bible: "Who knoweth whether thou art come to the kingdom for such a time as this?" (Es. 4:14) He wanted her to face the possibility that this might be the greatest opportunity of her life.

Mordecai's challenging question set Esther free from her fears. Not willing to miss God's will for her life, she laid her future on the line, announcing she was going in to see the king on behalf of her people, saying, "If I perish, I perish" (Es. 4:16). As a result of her intercession, the Jews were spared. Esther had indeed come to the kingdom for that crucial time.

And who knows whether you have come to the kingdom for such a time as this?

You may be God's person of the hour.

Perhaps you are the key to revival in your church, the reaching of your community for Christ, a spiritual and moral awakening in the nation. This may be the occasion for which you were born. How sad to miss God's best because of doubts, bitterness, an unforgiving heart, or some other negative attitude!

Doubt your doubts.

Believe your beliefs.

Press forward in faith.

You're positively dynamite.

12

Do Something!

A major league baseball player stands in the on-deck circle, swinging a bat. The bat has a weighted ring on it, making it heavier and harder to swing than would normally be the case. When his time at bat arrives, he strikes the bat handle on the ground and the weighted ring falls off. Then he makes his way to the plate where he will swing a bat that feels lighter because the added weight is gone.

Losing a negative attitude is something like that.

Losing Weights

During the closing service of a series of meetings where I had been speaking about total surrender to the Lord, a woman stood to tell what God had been doing in her life that week. "The bitterness is gone," she said. Her relief was evident, and it was easy to see that she had been set free from negative feelings that had been dragging her down and taking away the joy of living.

Runners dress as lightly as possible so that they will not be slowed by unneeded weight. The writer of Hebrews says we ought to follow this principle in the race of life, explaining: "Wherefore seeing we also are compassed about with so great a cloud of witnesses, let us lay aside every weight, and the sin which doth so easily beset us, and let us run with patience the race that is set before us" (Heb. 12:1).

Some negative attitudes are clearly sinful; others might be called weights. In either case, they hinder us in contending for the prize at the end of the race.

Reviewing Positive Principles

Perhaps understanding that God really cares about you has enabled you to jettison some feelings that had been troubling you for a long time. You had become problem conscious, but now you are focusing on the mighty power of God. Faith has replaced fear and that cloud of depression that had kept the sunlight from your path has lifted. You feel as if you've been given a new lease on life.

During our time together, you've come to realize something of the value of time and have decided to stop wasting hours being bitter and down when you could be using them positively to do meaningful things. Starting each day looking for the most profitable ways to invest your valuable time has added adventure and optimism to your life.

Though you still have many unpaid bills, you have gained a degree of freedom from the money blues, being convinced that you can't afford them. Perhaps just standing back and taking a fresh look at your financial condition in the light of God's boundless resources has brought needed relief and an increase of your faith. You may even be considering some additional giving to see how the law of sowing and reaping affects your financial situation when you use it biblically and with much prayer.

Some of your friends have improved personalities. Well, at least they appear to be better people since you've stopped specializing in faultfinding. You're happier with your family and with the family of God now that you're looking for positive things in people, rather than focusing on their weaknesses. And others seem to enjoy your company more than they did before.

Learning to stay positive has not ended your troubles, but it has changed your attitude toward them. Remembering that Jesus also endured severe trials and that He did so without complaining has caused you to think of life's difficulties in a different light. You've known for a long time that all trials are temporary, but for some reason you reacted as if they were here to stay. Giving more thought to what lies ahead for you as a believer has lessened the pain of the present, enabling you now to keep in mind that the best is yet to come.

Closing the door on the past has been hard for you. Voices of old sins, confessed long ago, had refused to be silent. Though forgiven, you were haunted by memories of the past. Now you know how unfounded those fears about not being totally forgiven have been. You see the wisdom of forgetting the things that are behind, and you've decided to do so. Old grudges have been put away. As much as possible, old failures have been forgotten. You're looking upward and onward, expecting great tomorrows.

Contentment had been something you read about in the lives of others; something that belonged to the smilers. It had eluded you. Now you've been taking stock of all your blessings and realize that you're really a wealthy person. You see that you had required too much to make you thankful and had allowed trifles to get you down. Just being thankful to be alive each morning and appreciating things that you had been taking for granted has added a whole new dimension to living.

Proper care of your body, God's temple, has also made a difference. Somehow you had never associated irregular hours and a junk food diet with your negativism. Discovering that health and happiness are closely related has been a lesson worth learning. You're feeling better too.

Accepting your great potential has been a little difficult. You had settled for mediocrity and find it hard to break out of that thinking pattern. But you've opened the door to greater things by telling the Lord that you're willing to do whatever pleases Him and that as best you know you are taking off the limits of usefulness, allowing Him in His wisdom to begin expanding your borders if that is His will for your life.

The reprogramming that you started shortly after beginning this study is continuing. Shutting out some of the negative input was tough at first because you had become so used to your old lifestyle but each day it has become a bit easier. Filling the void with things that fit Paul's call to think on things of virtue and praise and that are of good report was quite an order, but with the passing of time you are finding ways to do so.

Helping Others

Now that your negativism is fading and your thoughts are conforming to Paul's positive pattern given in Philippians 4:8, you are ready
to enter the most productive time of your life. God has not delivered
you from bitterness and depression just so that you can feel better.
He wants to use the new you to help others who are down. Paul
revealed this in 2 Corinthians 1:3-4, writing: "Blessed be God, even
the Father of our Lord Jesus Christ, the Father of mercies, and the
God of all comfort, who comforteth us in all our tribulation, that we
may be able to comfort them which are in any trouble, by the comfort
wherewith we ourselves are comforted of God."

* * *

The elderly man who was praying in our midweek service was one
of those special people who seem always to be filled with praise and
thanksgiving. During the summer, he frequently attended the services of my first church, but a good share of the year he traveled
about the country, witnessing to others about his faith in Christ.
Tonight, as he prayed, he asked the Lord to bless me as pastor. "O
Lord," he said, "bless the pastor, for no man can be a blessing to
others unless he himself is blessed of God."

For me, both that prayer and the principle it stated have been
unforgettable. The prayer was an honest, heartfelt cry for God's
blessing upon my ministry. The principle was that when that blessing
came I would be able to share it with others. This good and faithful
man was not asking his Lord to bless me so that I would feel good
or do well just for my own benefit, but so that I could be a blessing
to those in need.

A woman called who was in deep despair. Though I had never met
her, she had called because my name had been given to her as one
who might be able to help her with her problems. This Christian wife
and mother was so down that she felt there was no way out of her
dark valley.

Sensing her feeling of hopelessness, I slipped to my knees and
prayed for her while listening to her sad story. After she had finished
pouring out her troubles, I shared some thoughts from the Bible with
her, relating them to her problems, and then had prayer with her over
the phone. More counseling and prayer followed.

Within a short time, her darkness began departing. She made a new commitment to Christ and became active in a church. But there is more. Not content to just bask in God's blessings, she began helping others who were hurting. Eventually, she became involved in ministering to many troubled people, some of whom faced problems similar to those she had come through.

Positive people reach out to others.

If you do not use your new positive outlook, you will lose it.

The New You

Those nearest and dearest to you should be the first beneficiaries of your changed attitude. If you have been critical, bitter, or cold in your home, this is the perfect place to demonstrate the reality of your new approach to life. Note how this pattern is followed in Ephesians 5:18-33. Immediately after telling his readers to be filled with the Spirit, Paul explains how this should affect their home life.

Become the encourager in your family.

Show affection to those you have neglected in the past.

Be as quick to be thankful as you once were to complain.

Seize opportunities to express love.

Let family members know that you believe in them and that you expect the best from them.

Your church should also feel the impact of your change to positive living. If you have been given to griping, let your life be characterized by praise. If you have been known as the hold-back on new projects, cultivate a reputation for courage to move forward in faith. If you have been a divider of the congregation, become a peacemaker.

Give the devil trouble instead of your pastor.

Expect people to be converted through your pastor's ministry. Lead others to Christ and bring them to your pastor for instruction in Christian growth. When others criticize your pastor, defend him and emphasize his strong points. Pray for him and urge others to do the same.

Seek to see the world through the eyes of Jesus. Pray for the kind of urgency about reaching lost people that He demanded in John 4:35: "Say not ye, There are yet four months, and then cometh harvest? Behold, I say unto you, Lift up your eyes, and look on the fields, for they are white already unto harvest."

Cut through the maze of excuses that have kept you from getting involved in reaching people for Christ in your community. Let Ecclesiastes 11:4 become your excuse destroyer: "He that observeth the wind shall not sow; and he that regardeth the clouds shall not reap."

Volunteer for Christian service. Join the choir. Offer to teach a Sunday School class. Accept the next position offered you. Start a prayer group. Dedicate your car to the Lord and use it to transport people to church. Sponsor a youth group. Ask your pastor if you can have some job that no one else wants.

Abdicate your position as the chief complainer at work. Smile at minor irritations and thank the Lord for them. Stop worrying about others taking advantage of you. See the Lord's hand in times of stress that once would have caused you to fret or fight: "Let your light so shine before men, that they may see your good works, and glorify your Father which is in heaven" (Matt. 5:16).

I once led a carpenter to Christ. The next day he hit his thumb with his hammer. "Praise the Lord!" he said. The other workmen could hardly believe what they heard. But they knew that there was a different man among them.

The world takes notice of believers who are different.

Too often, however, we have only been noticed for our negativism. We are known for what we do not do. How many do you know who are known for their positive reactions to persecution and slander?

Give thanks the next time you have an opportunity to live out the positive reaction commanded in Matthew 5:11-12: "Blessed are ye when men shall revile you, and persecute you, and shall say all manner of evil against you falsely for my sake. Rejoice and be exceeding glad, for great is your reward in heaven; for so persecuted they the prophets which were before you."

Tackle the project that you have long wanted to do but have lacked the courage. Start that painting. Write that poem or compose that song. Launch that "someday-I'm-going-to" dream. Even if your first try doesn't come up to your expectations, you will have made an effort to put your idea into action. If you find that you don't have a natural bent to the project you've been dreaming about, you can find a new dream. But you may do very well and this may lead on to greater things. You will never know unless you try.

Gaining by Giving

Do something for others.

Help somebody.

Read the story of the Good Samaritan (Luke 10:30-37) and see how you can apply it in your own neighborhood.

Prepare some food for a sick friend.

During my wife's long illness, mentioned earlier, Christian friends from our church organized to care for our dinner each day. Every afternoon for six weeks, someone came to our door with a hot meal for our family. How grateful we were for this demonstration of Christian love.

You will be helped by helping others. Tim LaHaye says:

> The most rewarding and gratifying experiences in life come in serving people. This will be emotionally therapeutic. Depressed people are inclined to spend too much time thinking about themselves. Serving God by helping people forces you to think about someone besides yourself. I am personally convinced that God has oriented the human psyche in such a way that unless a man befriends others, he cannot be satisfied with himself. The rewards of such service are not only beneficial for eternity, but also helpful in this life.[1]

So in giving you will gain; in aiding others you will be enriched.

Throw yourself into a worthy cause.

William Wilberforce was greatly influenced by the ministry of John Wesley. The consuming passion of his life was to bring an end to slavery in the British Empire. But he appeared to be one of the most unlikely men in England to accomplish it.

Wilberforce had plenty of reasons to be negative about his chances of success. One of the most noticeable of these was his poor health. A writer of that era spoke of his "twisted body." Nevertheless, he became convinced that God had given him the task of freeing Britain's slaves, and he set out to do it.

Slavery was very profitable, and most of Britain's leaders did not want it to end. Had it not been for his faith in God, Wilberforce would have given up in the face of this powerful opposition; but he was sure that God's power was greater than that of his foes.

Though he did not live to see the battle completely won, on the day of Wilberforce's funeral, the British Parliament passed a law freeing all the slaves in the Empire. The man with the frail body had been successful in his crusade for freedom against immense political power. He had demonstrated that faith is the victory that overcomes the world (1 John 5:4).

A Task Just for Positive You

There is some task in your world for which you are better equipped than anyone else. Why not get involved?

We've got enough experts at faultfinding.

We need some doers.

Paul pictured himself as an athlete. Physically, he didn't fit that image. But to him the greatest contest was life. He seized each day as a never returning opportunity and called on his hearers and readers to make the most of every moment. He must have practiced what he preached, for no one could have coasted through life and equalled his accomplishments. Even the leaders of the mighty Roman Empire could not ignore him. Capsulizing his own lifestyle, he recommended this simple but powerful formula: "And whatsoever ye do, do it heartily as to the Lord, and not unto men" (Col. 3:23).

So, what needs fixing in your church, your community, the nation, even the world? How long have you been stewing about it? Have you thought yourself inadequate? Those feelings belong to your past, your negative days. Remember Wilberforce and other heroes of the faith and the source of their strength.

Share your concern with your pastor or some other person in whom you have confidence and offer to get involved and become part of a positive solution.

Do something . . . today!

Footnotes

Chapter 1

1. Dale Carnegie, *How to Stop Worrying and Start Living,* Simon and Schuster, New York, 1948, Pocket Books, Inc., New York, 1953, p. 320.

2. Craig Massey, *Moody Monthly,* Chicago, April, 1974.

3. *The Pulpit Commentary,* Funk & Wagnalls Company, London and New York, Vol. 16, p. 47.

4. J.C. Ryle, *Holiness,* Fleming H. Revell, Old Tappan, N.J., p. 197.

5. Walter B. Knight, *Knight's Master Book of Illustrations,* Wm. B. Eerdmans Publishing Co., Grand Rapids, Michigan, 1956, p. 52.

6. G.B. Hardy, *Countdown,* Moody Press, Chicago, 1972, p. 52.

7. Ibid., p. 51.

8. Herbert Lockyer, *Dark Threads the Weaver Needs,* Fleming H. Revell, Old Tappan, N.J., 1979, p. 60.

9. Walter B. Knight, *Knight's Master Book of New Illustrations,* Wm. B. Eerdmans Publishing Company, Grand Rapids, Michigan, 1956, p. 641.

10. Herbert Lockyer, *Dark Threads the Weaver Needs,* Fleming H. Revell, Old Tappan, N.J., 1979, p. 76.

Chapter 2

1. Walter B. Knight, *Knight's Treasury of Illustrations,* Wm. B. Eerdmans Publishing Company, Grand Rapids, Michigan, 1963, p. 115.

2. Roger F. Campbell, Article in *Certainty,* Regular Baptist Press, Schaumburg, Illinois, Dec. 4, 1983 issue.

3. Robert V. Ozment, *But God Can,* Fleming H. Revell Company, Old Tappan, N.J., 1962, p. 117.

4. Walter B. Knight, *Knight's Master Book of New Illustrations,* Wm. B. Eerdmans Publishing Company, Grand Rapids, Michigan, 1956, p. 418.

5. John R. Rice, *Prayer—Asking and Receiving,* Sword of the Lord Publishers, 1942, p. 165.

6. Walter B. Knight, *Knight's Master Book of New Illustrations,* Wm. B. Eerdmans Publishing Company, Grand Rapids, Michigan, 1956, p. 187.

7. Roger F. Campbell, *Let's Communicate,* Christian Literature Crusade, Fort Washington, Pennsylvania, 1978, p. 176.

Chapter 3

1. Walter B. Knight, *Knight's Master Book of New Illustrations,* Wm. B. Eerdmans Publishing Company, Grand Rapids, Michigan, 1956, p. 139.

2. Tim LaHaye, *How to Win over Depression,* Zondervan Publishing House, Grand Rapids, Michigan, 1974, p. 203.

3. R.A. Torrey, *How to Pray,* Moody Press, Chicago, p. 24.

4. A.W. Tozer, *Man, the Dwelling Place of God,* Christian Publications, Harrisburg, Pennsylvania, 1966, p. 69.

Chapter 4

1. Tim LaHaye, *How to Win over Depression,* Zondervan Publishing House, Grand Rapids, Michigan, 1974, p. 104.

2. Ray C. Stedman, *Secrets of the Spirit,* Fleming H. Revell Company, Old Tappan, New Jersey, 1975, pp. 38-39.

3. Craig Massey, *Moody Monthly,* Chicago, April 1974.

4. Walter B. Knight, *Knight's Treasury of Illustrations,* Wm. B. Eerdmans Publishing Company, Grand Rapids, Michigan, 1963, p. 407.

5. John Edmund Haggai, *How to Win over Worry,* Zondervan Publishing House, Grand Rapids, Michigan, 1959, p. 83.

6. Walter B. Knight, *Knight's Treasury of Illustrations,* Wm. B. Eerdmans Publishing Company, Grand Rapids, Michigan, 1963, p. 407.

7. Walter B. Knight, *Knight's Master Book of New Illustrations,* Wm. B. Eerdmans Publishing Company, Grand Rapids, Michigan, 1956, p. 684.

8. John Edmund Haggai, *How to Win over Worry,* Zondervan Publishing House, Grand Rapids, Michigan, 1959, p. 84.

9. Ibid., p. 85.

10. Ted W. Engstrom & Alec Mackenzie, *Managing Your Time,* Zondervan Publishing House, Grand Rapids, Michigan, 1967, pp. 61-62.

11. Walter B. Knight, *Knight's Treasury of Illustrations,* Wm. B. Eerdmans Publishing Company, Grand Rapids, Michigan, 1963, p. 189.

12. John R. Rice, *God's Cure for Anxious Care,* Sword of the Lord Publishers, Murfreesboro, Tennessee, 1948, p. 19.

Chapter 5

1. Dale Carnegie, *How to Stop Worrying and Start Living,* Simon and Schuster, New York, 1948, Pocket Books, Inc. Edition, New York, 1953, p. 320.

2. S.I. McMillen, M.D., *None of These Diseases,* Fleming H. Revell Company, Old Tappan, New Jersey, 1963, pp. 128-129.

3. S.I. McMillen, M.D., *None of These Diseases,* Fleming H. Revell Company, Old Tappan, New Jersey, 1963, pp. 82-83.

4. Edgar A. Guest, *Today and Tomorrow,* The Reilly & Lee Company, Chicago, 1942. Copyright now held by Contemporary Books, Inc., Chicago.

Chapter 6

1. Walter B. Knight, *Knight's Master Book of New Illustrations*, Wm. B. Eerdmans Publishing Company, Grand Rapids, Michigan, 1956, p. 89.

2. From *Pulpit Helps*, Chattanooga, Tennessee, March, 1982 issue.

Chapter 7

1. Walter B. Knight, *Knight's Master Book of New Illustrations*, Wm. B. Eerdmans Publishing Company, Grand Rapids, Michigan, 1956, p. 184.

2. Shirley Lyon as told to Roger F. Campbell, *Power for Living*, Scripture Press Publications, Wheaton, Illinois, August 23, 1970.

3. Edward E. Powell, Jr., as told to Roger F. Campbell, *Turning Points*, Biographies, Inc., Bonita Springs, Florida, 1984.

4. Dr. John R. Rice, *God's Cure for Anxious Care*, Sword of the Lord Publishers, Murfreesboro, Tennessee, 1948, p.18.

5. Roger F. Campbell, *She Runs a Good Race, FreeWay*, Scripture Press Publications, Wheaton, Illinois, June 1, 1975.

6. Herbert Lockyer, *Dark Threads the Weaver Needs*, Fleming H. Revell Company, Old Tappan, New Jersey, 1979, p. 104.

Chapter 8

1. J.C. Ryle, *Holiness*, Fleming H. Revell, Old Tappan, New Jersey, p. 173.

2. Vance Havner, *Three Score & Ten*, Fleming H. Revell, Old Tappan, New Jersey, 1973, p. 72.

3. A.W. Tozer, *The Root of the Righteous*, Christian Publications, Inc., Harrisburg, Pennsylvania, 1955, p. 55.

Chapter 9

1. Dale Carnegie, *How to Stop Worrying and Start Living*, Simon and Schuster, New York, 1948, Pocket Books, Inc. Edition, New York, 1953, p. 131.

2. Alan Redpath, *Victorious Christian Living*, Fleming H. Revell Company, Old Tappan, New Jersey, 1955, p. 207.

Chapter 10

1. Bruce Larson, *There's a Lot More to Health than Not Being Sick,* Word Books, Waco, Texas, 1981, p. 123.

2. Roger F. Campbell, *Weight! A Better Way to Lose,* Victor Books, Wheaton, Illinois, 1976, pp. 13-14.

3. Bruce Larson, *There's a Lot More to Health than Not Being Sick,* Word Books, Waco, Texas, 1981, p. 75.

Chapter 11

1. R.A. Torrey, *Why God Used D.L. Moody,* Fleming H. Revell Company, Old Tappan, New Jersey, 1923, p. 10.

2. A.W. Tozer, *Man: The Dwelling Place of God,* Christian Publications, Inc., Harrisburg, Pennsylvania, 1966, p. 9.

3. Leslie B. Flynn, *19 Gifts of the Spirit,* Victor Books, Wheaton, Illinois, 1974, p. 194.

Chapter 12

1. Tim LaHaye, *How to Win over Depression,* Zondervan Publishing House, Grand Rapids, Michigan, 1974, p. 206.